MY LADY OF THE CHINESE COURTYARD

MORE WILDSIDE CLASSICS

Please see www.wildsidepress.com for a complete list!

MY LADY OF THE CHINESE COURTYARD

ELIZABETH COOPER

WILDSIDE PRESS

Dedicated to my husband.

MY LADY OF THE CHINESE COURTYARD

This edition published in 2006 by Wildside Press, LLC.
www.wildsidepress.com

AUTHOR'S NOTE

In these letters I have drawn quite freely and sometimes literally from the excellent and authoritative translations of Chinese classics by Professor Giles in his "Chinese Literature" and from "The Lute of Jude" and "The Mastersingers of Japan," two books in the "Wisdom of the East" series edited by L. Cranmer-Byng and S. A. Kapadia (E. P. Dutton and Company). These translators have loved the songs of the ancient poets of China and Japan and caught with sympathetic appreciation, in their translations, the spirit of the East.

I wish to thank them for their help in making it possible to render into English the poetry used by "My Lady of the Chinese Courtyard."

—Elizabeth Cooper.

Part 1

PREFACE

A writer on things Chinese was asked why one found so little writing upon the subject of the women of China. He stopped, looked puzzled for a moment, then said, "The woman of China! One never hears about them. I believe no one ever thinks about them, except perhaps that they are the mothers of the Chinese men!"

Such is the usual attitude taken in regard to the woman of the flowery Republic. She is practically unknown, she hides herself behind her husband and her sons, yet, because of that filial piety, that almost religious veneration in which all men of Eastern races hold their parents, she really exerts an untold influence upon the deeds of the men of her race.

Less is known about Chinese women than about any other women of Oriental lands. Their home life is a sealed book to the average person visiting China. Books about China deal mainly with the lower-class Chinese, as it is chiefly with that class that the average visitor or missionary comes into contact. The tourists see only the coolie woman bearing burdens in the street, trotting along with a couple of heavy baskets swung from her shoulders, or they stop to stare at the neatly dressed mothers sitting on their low stools in the narrow alleyways, patching clothing or fondling their children. They see and hear the boat-women, the women who have the most freedom of any in all China, as they weave their sampans in and out of the crowded traffic on the canals. These same tourists visit the tea-houses and see the gaily dressed "sing-song" girls, or catch a glimpse of a gaudily painted face, as a lady is hurried along in her sedan-chair, carried on the shoulders of her chanting bearers. But the real Chinese woman, with her hopes, her fears, her romances, her children, and her religion, is still undiscovered.

I hope that this book, based on letters shown me many years after they were written, will give a faint idea of the life of a Chinese lady. The story is told in two series of letters conceived to be written by Kwei-li, the wife of a very high Chinese official, to her husband when he accompanied his master, Prince Chung, on his trip around the world.

She was the daughter of a viceroy of Chih-li, a man most advanced for his time, who was one of the forerunners of the present educational movement in China, a movement which has caused her youth to rise and demand Western methods and Western enterprise in place of the obsolete traditions and customs of their ancestors. To show his belief in the new spirit that was breaking over his country, he educated his daughter along with his sons. She was given as tutor Ling-Wing-pu, a famous poet of his province, who doubtless taught her the imagery and beauty of expression which is so truly Eastern.

Within the beautiful ancestral home of her husband, high on the mountains-side outside of the city of Su-Chau, she lived the quite, sequestered life of the high-class Chinese woman, attending to the household duties, which are not light in these patriarchal homes, where an incredible number of people live under the same rooftree. The sons bring their wives to their father's house instead of establishing separate homes for themselves, and they are all under the watchful eye of the mother, who can make a veritable prison or a palace for her daughters-in-law. In China the mother reigns supreme.

The mother-in-law of Kwei-li was an old-time conservative Chinese lady, the woman who cannot adapt herself to the changing conditions, who resents change of methods, new interpretations and fresh expressions of life. She sees in the new ideas that her sons bring from the foreign schools disturbers only of her life's ideals. She instinctively feels that they are gathering about her retreat, beating at her doors, creeping in at her closely shuttered windows, even winning her sons from her arms. She stands an implacable foe of progress and she will not admit that the world is moving on, broadening its outlook and clothing itself in a new expression. She feels that she is being left behind with her dead gods, and she cries out against the change which is surely but slowly coming to China, and especially to Chinese women, with the advent of education and the knowledge of the outside world.

In a household in China a daughter-in-law is of very little importance until she is the mother of a son. Then, from being practically a servant of her husband's mother, she rises to place of equality and is looked upon with respect. She has fulfilled her once great duty, the thing for which she was created: she has given her husband a son to worship at his grave and at the graves of his ancestors. The great prayer which rises from the heart of all Chinese women, rich and poor, peasant and princess, is to Kwan-yin, for the inestimable blessing of sons. "Sons! Give me sons!" is heard in every temple. To be childless is the greatest sorrow that can come to Chinese women, as she fully realizes that for this cause her husband is justified in putting her away for another wife, and she may not complain or cry out, except in secret, to her Goddess of Mercy, who has not answered her prayers. Understanding this, we can dimly realise the joy of Kwei-li upon the birth of her son, and her despair upon his death.

At this time, when she was in very depths of despondency, when she had turned from the gods of her people, when it was feared that her sorrow, near to madness, she would take the little round ball of sleep— opium— that was brought rest to so many despairing women in China, her servants brought her the Gospel of St. John, which they bought of an itinerant colporteur in the market-place, hoping that it might interest her. In the long nights when sleep would not come to her, she read it— and found the peace she sought.

1

My Dear One,

The house on the mountain-top has lost its soul. It is nothing but a palace with empty windows. I go upon the terrace and look over the valley where the sun sinks a golden red ball, casting long purple shadows on the plain. Then I remember that thou art not coming from the city to me, and I stay to myself that there can be no dawn that I care to see, and no sunset to gladden my eyes, unless I share it with thee.

But do not think I am unhappy. I do everything the same as if thou wert here, and in everything I say, "Would this please my master?" Meh-ki wished to put thy long chair away, as she said it was too big; but I did not permit. It must rest where I can look at it and imagine I see thee lying it, smoking thy water pipe; and the small table is always near by, where thou canst reach out thy hand for thy papers and the drink thou lovest. Meh-ki also brought out the dwarf pine-tree and put it on the terrace, but I remembered thou saidst it looked like an old man who had been beaten in his childhood, and I gave it to her for one of the inner courtyards. She thinks it very beautiful, and so I did once; but I have learned to see with thine eyes, and I know now that a tree made straight and beautiful and tall by the Gods is more to be regarded than one that has been bent and twisted by man.

Such a long letter I am writing thee. I am so glad that though madest me promise to write thee every seventh day, and to tell thee all that passes within my household and my heart. Thine Honourable Mother says it is not seemly to send communication from mine hand to thine. She says it was a thing unheard of in her girlhood, and that we younger generations have passed the limits of all modesty and womanliness. She wishes me to have the writer or thy brother send thee the news of thine household; but that I will not permit. It must come from me, thy wife. Each one of these strokes will come to thee bearing my message. Thou wilt not tear the covering roughly as thou didst those great official letters; nor wilt thou crush the papers quickly in thy hand, because it is the written word of Kwei-li, who sends with each stroke of brush a part of her heart.

2

My Dear One,

My first letter to thee was full of sadness and longing because thou wert newly gone from me. Now a week has passed, the sadness is still in my heart, but it is buried deep for only me to know. I have my duties which must be done, my daily tasks that only I can do since thine Honourable Mother has handed me the keys of the rice-bin. I realise the great honour she does me, and that at last she trusts me and believes me no child as she did when I first entered her household.

Can I ever forget that day when I came to my husband's people? I had the one great consolation of a bride, my parents had not sent me away empty-handed. The procession was almost a li in length and I watched with a swelling heart the many tens of coolies carrying my household goods. There were the silken coverlets for the beds, and they were folded to show their richness and carried on red lacquered tables of great value. There were the household utensils of many kinds, the vegetable dishes, the baskets, the camphor-wood baskets containing my clothing, tens upon tens of them; and I said within my heart as they passed me by, "Enter my new home before me. Help me find a loving welcome." Then at the end of the chanting procession I came in my red chair of marriage, so closely covered I could barely breathe. My trembling feet could scarce support me as they helped me from the chair, and my hand shook with fear as I was being led into my new household. She stood bravely before you, that little girl dressed in red and gold, her hair twined with pearls and jade, her arms tiny finger, but with all her bravery she was frightened—frightened. She was away from her parents for the first time, away from all who love her, and she knew if she did not meet with approval in her new home her rice-bowl would be full of bitterness for many moons to come.

After the obeisance to the ancestral tablet and we had fallen upon our knees before thine Honourable Parent, I then saw for the first time the face of my husband. Dost thou remember when first thou raised my veil and looked long into my eyes? I was thinking, "Will he find me beautiful?" and in fear I could look but for a moment, then my eyes fell and I would not raise then to thine again. But in that moment I saw that thou wert tall and beautiful, that thine eyes were truly almond, that thy skin was clear and thy teeth like pearls. I was secretly glad within my heart, because I have known of brides who, when they saw their husbands for the first time, wished to scream in terror, as they were old or ugly. I thought to myself that I could be happy with this tall, strong young man if I found favour in his sight, and I said a little prayer to Kwan-yin. Because she has answered that prayer, each day I place a candle at her feet to show my gratitude.

I think thine Honourable Mother has passed me the keys of the household to take my mind from my loss. She says a heart that is busy cannot mourn, and my days are full of duties. I arise in the morning early, and after seeing that my hair is tidy, I take a cup of tea to the Aged One and make my obeisance; then I place the rice and water in their dishes before the God of the Kitchen, and light a tiny stick of incense for his altar, so that our day may begin auspiciously. After the morning meal I consult with the cook and steward. The vegetables must be regarded carefully and the fish inspected, and I must ask the price that has been paid, because often a hireling is hurried and forgets that a bargain is not made with a breath.

I carry the great keys and feel much pride when I open the door of the storeroom. Why, I do not know, unless it is because of the realisation that I am the head of this large household. If the servants or their children are ill, they come to me instead of to thine Honourable Mother, as they be too rare or heavy for one of my mind and experience.

Then I go with the gardener to the terrace and help him arrange the flowers for the day. I love the stone-flagged terrace, with its low marble balustrade, resting close against the mountain to which it seems to cling.

I always stop a moment and look over the valley, because it was from here I watched thee when thou went to the city in the morning, and here I waited thy return. Because of my love for it and the rope of remembrance with which it binds me, I keep it beautiful with rugs and flowers.

It speaks to me of happiness and brings back memories of summer days spent idling in a quite so still that we could hear the rustle of the bamboo grasses on the hillside down below; or, still more dear, the evenings passed close by thy side, watching the brightened into jade each door and archway as it passed.

I long for thee, I love thee, I am thine.

Thy Wife.

3

My Dear One,

The hours of one day are as like each other as are twin blossoms from the pear-tree. There is no news to tell thee. The mornings are passed in the duties that come to all women who have the care of a household, and the afternoons I am on the terrace with thy sister. But first of all, thine August Mother must be made comfortable for her sleep, and then the peace indeed is wonderful.

Mah-li and I take our embroidery and sit upon the terrace, where we pass long hours watching the people in the valley below. The faint blue smoke curls from a thousand dwellings, and we try to imagine the lives of those who dwell beneath the rooftrees. We see the peasants in their rice-fields; watch them dragging the rich mud from the bottoms of the canal for fertilizing; hear the shrill whistle of the duck man as, with long bamboo, he drives the great flock of ducks homeward or sends them over the fields to search for insects. We see the wedding procession far below, and can but faintly follow the great covered chair of the bride and the train of servants carrying the possessions to the new home. Often the wailing of the mourners in a funeral comes to our ears, and we lean far over the balcony to watch the coolie scatter the spirit money that will pay the dead man's way to land of the Gods. But yesterday we saw the procession carrying the merchant Wong to his resting-place of sycee spent upon his funeral. Thy brothers tell me his sons made great boast that no man has been buried with such pomp in all the province. But it only brings more clearly the remembrance that he began this life a sampan coolie and ended it with many millions. But his millions did not bring him happiness. He laboured without ceasing, and then without living to enjoy the fruit, worn out, departed, one knows not whither.

Yesterday we heard the clang-clang of a gong and saw the Taotai pass by, his men carrying the boards and banners with his official rank and virtues written upon them, and we counted the red umbrellas and wondered if some poor peasant was in deep trouble.

It is beautiful here now. The hillside is purple with the

autumn bloom and air is filled with a golden haze. The red leaves drift slowly down the canal and tell me that soon the winter winds will come. Outside the walls the insects sing sleepily in grass, seeming to know that their brief life is nearly spent. The wild geese on their southward flight carry my thoughts to thee. All is sad, and sad as the clouded moon my longing face, and my eyes are filled with tears. Not at twilight nor at grey of dawn can I find happiness without thee, my lord, mine own, and "endless are the days as trailing creepers."

Thy Wife.

4

My Dear One,

I have much to tell thee. My last letter was unhappy, and these little slips of paper must bring to thee joy, not sorrow, else why the written word?

First, I must tell thee that thy brother Chih-peh will soon be married. Thou knowest he has long been betrothed to Li-ti, the daughter of the Governor of Chih-li, and soon the bride will be here. We have been arranging her apartments. We do not know how many home servants she will bring, and we are praying the Gods to grant her discretion, because with servants from a different province there are sure to be jealousies and the retailing of small tales that disturb the harmony of a household.

Many tales have been brought us of her great beauty, and we hear she has much education. Thine August Mother is much disturbed over the latter, as she says, and justly too, that over-learning is not good for women. It is not meet to give them books in which to store their embroidery silks. But I— I am secretly delighted, and Mah-li, thy sister, is transported with joy. I think within our hearts, although we would not even whisper it to the night wind, we are glad that there will be three instead of two to bear the burden of the discourses of thine Honourable Mother. Not that she talks too much, thou understandest, nor that her speech is not stored full of wisdom, but— she talks— and we must listen.

We have other news. A new slave-girl has come into our household. As thou knowest, there has been a great famine to the north of us, and the boats, who follow all disaster, have been anchored in our canal. I do not know why August One desired to add one more to take of rice beneath our rooftree; but she is here. She was brought before me, a little peasant girl, dressed in faded blue trousers and a jacket that had been many times to the washing pool. Her black hair was coiled in the girlhood knot at the side of the head, and in it she had stuck a pumpkin blossom. She was such a pretty little country flower, and looked so helpless, I drew her to me and questioned her. She told me there were many within their compound wall: grandmother, father, mother, brothers, sisters, uncles and cousins. The rice was gone, the heavy clothing and all of value in the pawn-shop. Death was all around them, and they watched each day as he drew nearer— nearer. Then came the buyers of girls. They had money that would buy rice for the winter and mean life to all. But the mother would not listen. She was told over and over that the price of one would save the many. Her nights were spent in weeping and her days in fearful watching. At last, worn out, despairing, she went to a far-off temple to ask Kwan-yin, the Mother of Mercies, for help in her great trouble. While she was gone, Ho-tai was taken to the women in the boat at the water-gate, and many pieces of silver were paid the father. When the stomach is empty, pride is not strong, and there were many small bodies crying for rice that could only be bought with the sacrifice of one. That night, as they started down the canal, they saw on the tow-path a peasant women, her dress open far below her throat, her hair loose and flying, her eyes swollen and dry from over-weeping, moaning pitifully, stumbling on in the darkness, searching for the boat that had been anchored at the water-gate; but it was gone. Poor little Ho-tai! She said, "It was my mother!" and as she told me, he face was wet with bitter rain. I soothed her and told her we would make her happy, and I made a little vow in my heart that I would find that mother and bring peace to her heart again.

The summer wanes and autumn is upon us with all its mists and shadows of purple and grey. The camphor-trees look from the distance like great balls of fire, and the eucalyptus-tree, in its dress of brilliant yellow, is a gaily painted court lady. If one short glimpse of thee my heart could gladden, then all my soul would be filled with the beauty of this time, these days of red and gold. But now I seek thee the long night through, and turn to make my arm thy pillow— but thou art gone.

I am thy wife who longs for thee.

5

My Dear One,

We have a daughter-in-law. Not only have we a daughter-in-law, but we have servants and household furnishings and clothing— and clothing— and clothing. I am sure that if her gowns could be laid side by side, they would reach around the world. She is as fair as the spring blossoms, and of as little use. An army encamped upon us could not have so upset our household as the advent of this one maiden. She brought with her rugs to cover the floors, embroideries and hangings for the walls, scrolls and saying of Confucius and Mencius to hang over the seats of honour— to show us that she is an admirer of the classics— screens for the doorways, even a huge bed all carved and gilded and with hangings and tassels of gay silk.

Thine Honourable Mother, after viewing the goods piled in the courtyards, called her bearers and told us she was taking tea with a friend in the village of Sung-dong. I think she chose this friend because she lives the farthest from our compound walls. I alone was left to direct the placing of this furniture. Li-ti was like a butterfly, flitting hither and thither, doing nothing, talking much. The bed must be so placed that the Spirits of Evil passing over it in the night-time could not take the souls of sleepers away with them. The screens must stand at the proper angle guarding the doorways from the spirits who, in their straight, swift flight through the air, fall against these screens instead of entering the house. She gravely explained to me that the souls who dwell in darkness like to take up their abode in newly organised households, and many precautions must be made against them. She even seriously considered the roof, to see if all the points curved upward, so that the spirits lighting upon them be carried high above the open courtyards. I do not know what would have happened to thine ancestral rooftree if it had not met with her approval. I was many heartfuls glad that thine August Mother was taking tea in a far-off village, as Li-ti even wanted to install a new God in the kitchen. This I would not permit. Canst thou imagine thy Mother's face if a God from a stranger family was in the niche above the stove? Happily all was over when thine Honourable Mother returned. She is not pleased with this, her newest, daughter-in-law, and she talks— and talks— and talks. She says the days will pass most slowly until she sees the father of Li-ti. She yearns to tell him that a man knows how to spend a million pieces of money in marrying off his daughter, but knows not how to spend a hundred thousand in bringing up his child. If this great Governor of Chih-li has much wisdom, he will stay long within his province. I have just heard for the hundredth time the saying of Confucius, "Birth is not a beginning, nor is death an end." In my despair I said deep down within my breast, "I am sure it will not be an end for thee, O Mother-in-law. Thou wilt go to the River of Souls talking, talking, always talking— but the Gods will be good to me. Thou must pass before me, and I will not hasten so as to overtake thee on the way." I beg thy pardon, dear one. I lack respect to thy Most Honourable Parent, but my soul is sore tried and I can find no quite.

I am, Thy Wife.

6

My Dear One,

"The five worst infirmities that afflict the female are indocility, discontent, slander, jealousy, and silliness. The worst of them all, and the parent of the other four, is silliness. "Does that not sound familiar to thine ears? Life is serious here in thine ancestral home since we have taken to ourselves a daughter-in-law. The written word for trouble is two women beneath one roof-tree, and I greatly fear that the wise man who invented writing had knowledge that cost him dear. Perhaps he, too, had a daughter-in-law.

Yet, with it all, Li-ti is such a child. Ah, I see thee smile. Thou sayest she is only three years less in age than I; yet, thou seest, I have had the honour of living a year by the side of thy Most August Mother and have acquired much knowledge from the very fountain-head of wisdom. Perchance Li-ti also will become a sage, if— she be not gathered to her ancestors before her allotted time, which depends upon the strength of body and mind which they may have willed her.

To me she is the light of this old palace. She is the true spirit of laughter, and, "When the happy laugh, the Gods rejoice." She is continually in disgrace with thine Honourable Mother, and now the Elder One has decided that both she and Mah-li, thy sister, shall learn a text from the sage Confucius each day for penance. They are now in the inner courtyard, studying the six shadows which attend the six virtues. I can hear them saying over and over to each other, "Love of goodness without the will to learn casts the shadow called foolishness—" now a laugh— then again they begin, "Love of knowledge without the will to learn casts the shadow called instability—" giggle and much talking. I am afraid they will never arrive at the shadow cast the love of truth, and after I have written thee I will go in and help them, that they may not be reprimanded.

Li-ti takes her duties now most seriously, these same duties consisting of dressing for the day. In the morning she seats herself before her mirror, and two maids attend her, one to hold the great brass bowl of water, the other to hand her the implements of her toilet. While the face is warm she covers it with honey mixed with perfume, and applies the rice-powder until her face is as white as the rice itself. Then the cheeks are rouged, the touch of red is placed upon the lower lip, the eyebrows are shaped like the true willow leaf, and the hair is dressed. Her hair is wonderful (but I say within, my hearty not so long or so thick as mine), and she adorn it with many jewels of jade and pearls. Over her soft clothing of fine linen she draws the rich embroidered robes of silk and satin. Then her jewels, earrings, beads, bracelets, rings, the tiny mirror in the embroidered case, the bag with its rouge and powder fastened to her side by long red tassels. When all things are in place, she rises a being glorified, a thing of beauty from her glossy hair to the toe of her tiny embroidered shoe. I watch her with a little envy, because when thou wast here I did the same. Now that my husband is away, it is not meet that I make myself too seemly for other eyes. The rouge brush and the powder have not been near my face, and I have searched my clothing chests to find gowns fitting for a woman who is alone.

Thy Mother says poor Li-ti is o'ervain, and repeats to her the saying, "More precious in a woman is a virtuous heart than a face of beauty." But I say she is our butterfly, she brings the joys of summer. One must not expect a lace kerchief to hold tears, and she fulfills her woman's destiny. Chih-peh, thy brother, is inexpressibly happy. He adores his pretty blossom. He follows her with eyes worship, and when she is in disgrace with thine August Mother, he is desolate. When needs be she is sent to her apartment, he wanders round and round the courtyards until the Honourable One has retired from sight, then he hurriedly goes to his beloved. Soon I hear them laughing gaily, and know the storm is over.

The rains have come and we cannot pass long days upon the terrace. The whole valley is shrouded in grey mists and the peasants have gone from the fields. The path down the mountain-side is empty, except for the men with the great umbrella hats and capes of straw, bringing the vegetables to the monastery below. The old abbot of the monastery is in great trouble. Some men have come and wish to erect long poles with wires on them. It is feared it will interrupt the feng-shui of the temple, the good spirits of the air cannot pass, and will rest upon these ugly poles instead of coming to the temple rooftree. The abbot has wailed and gone to the magistrate; but he will not interfere, as the men have many tens of thousands of sycee and quite likely will work their will.

Such foolish letters as I write thee! They are filled with the little life that passes within the women's courtyard. It is all the life I know. My world is bounded by these walls, and I ask no more.

I am thy loving wife.

7

My Dear One,

All thy women-folk have been shopping! A most unheard-of event for us. We have Li-ti to thank for this great pleasure, because, but for her, the merchants would have brought their goods to the courtyard for us to make our choice. Li-ti would not hear of that; she wanted to see the city, and she wanted to finger the pretty goods within the shops. She knew exactly what she wished, and life was made uncomfortable for us all until thy Mother ordered the chairs and we went into the city. We were a long procession. First, the August One with her four-bearer chair; then your most humble wife, who has only two bearers— as yet; then Li-ti; and after her Mah-li, followed by the chairs of the servants who came to carry back our purchases.

It was most exciting for us all, as we go rarely within the city gate. It was market day and the streets were made more narrow by the baskets of fish and vegetables which lined the way. The flat stones of the pavements were slippery and it seemed our bearers could not find a way amongst the crowd of riders on horses and small donkeys, the coolies with their buckets of hot water swinging from their shoulders, the sweetmeat sellers, the men with bundles, and the women with small baskets. They all stepped to one side at the sound of the Ah-yo of our leader, except a band of coolies carrying the monstrous trunk of a pine-tree, chanting as they swung the mast between them, and keeping step with the chant. It seemed a solemn dirge, as if some great were being carried to the resting-place of the dead.

But sadness could not come to us when shopping, and our eager eyes looked long at the signs above the open shopways. There were long black signs of lacquer with letters of raised gold, or red ones with the characters carved and gilded. Above a shoe-shop was a made for the King of the Mountains, in front of a pipe-shop was a water pipe fit for his mate. From the fan-shop hung delicate, gilded fans; and framing the silk-shop windows gaily coloured silk was draped in rich festoons that nearly swept the pathway.

We bought silks and satins and gay brocades, we chatted and we bargained and we shopped. We handled jade and pearls and ornaments of twisted gold, and we priced amulets and incense pots and gods. We filled our eyes with luxury and our amahs' chairs with packages, and returned home three happy, tired, hungry women, thinking with longing of the hissing tea-urn upon the charcoal brazier.

That crowded, bustling, threatening city seems another world from this, our quiet, walled-in dwelling. I feel that here we are protected, cared for, guarded, and life's hurry and distress will only pass us by, not touch us. Yet— we like to see it all, and know that we are part of that great wonder-thing, the world.

I am thy happy, tired, Wife.

8

My Dear One,

I am carrying a burden for another that is causing me much sorrow. Dost thou remember Chen-peh, who is from my province and who married Ling Peh-yu about two moons after I came to thy household? She came to me yesterday in dire distress. She is being returned to her home by her husband's people, and, as thou knowest, if a woman is divorced shame covers her until her latest hour. I am inexpressibly saddened, as I do not know what can be done. The trouble is with his mother and, I fear, her own pride of family. She cannot forget that she comes from a great house, and she is filled with pride at the recollection of her home. I have told her that the father and mother of one's husband should be honoured beyond her own. I can see that she has failed in respect; and thus she merits condemnation. We have all learned as babes that "respect" is the first word in the book of wisdom. I know it is hard at times to still the tongue, but all paths that lead to peace are hard.

She will remain with me two nights. Last night she lay wide-eyed, staring into the darkness, with I know not what within her soul. I begged her to think wisely, to talk frankly with her husband and his mother, to whom she owes obedience. There should be no pride where love is. She must think upon the winter of her days, when she will be alone without husband and without children, eating bitter rice of charity, though 'tis given by her people. I put her in remembrance of that saying of the poet:

"Rudely torn may be a cotton mantle, yet a skillful hand may join it; Snapped may be the string where pearls are threaded, yet the thread all swiftly knotted; But a husband and his wife, once parted, never more may meet."

I must not bring thee the sorrows of another. Oh, dear one, there will never come 'twixt thee and me the least small river of distrust. I will bear to thee no double heart, and thou wilt cherish me and love me always.

Thy Wife.

9

My Dear One,

I cannot wait until the seventh day to write thee again, as my letter to thee yestereve was full of sadness and longing. Now I have slept, and troubles from a distance do not seem so grave.

Thine Honourable Mother has chided me gravely, but to my mind unjustly, and, as thou knowest, I could not answer her words, though they pierced me "like arrows from the strings of white-winged bows." Poor Li-ti is in trouble again, and this time she has brought it upon herself, yet she cannot he blamed. I as the head of the household, as thine Honourable Mother has told me, should have protected her. I told thee that she brought servants from her old home, and amongst them her childhood's nurse, who, I am sure, loves Li-ti dearly; but, as many women who have little to occupy their hands, she loves to sit in the women's court-yard and gossip. If it had stopped within the servants' courtyard all would have been well; but at the time of Li-ti's dressing all the small goods she had gathered during the day were emptied into the lap of Li-ti, who is too young to know that "as poison that reaches the blood spreads through the body, so does the love of gossip spread through the soul of woman." I do not know how it came about, but comparisons were made between the house-holds, that of her home and that of her husband, and news was carried back to the servants' quarters until at last our household was in a state of unrest that stopped all work and made living quite impossible.

It seems small, but it is the retailing of little calumnies that dis-turbs the harmony of kinsmen and ruins the peace of families. Finally I found it necessary to talk to Li-ti's nurse, and I told her many things it were good for her to know. I warned her that if she did not wish to revisit her home province she must still her tongue. Things were better for a time, but they commenced again, and I called her to my courtyard and said to her, "The sheaves of rice have been beaten across the wood for the last time. You must go." Li-ti was inconsolable, but I was firm. Such quarrels are not becoming when we are so many beneath one rooftree.

The servant went away, but she claimed her servant's right of reviling us within our gate. She lay beneath our outer archway for three long hours and called down curses upon the Liu family. One could not get away from the sound of the enumeration of the faults and vices of thy illustrious ancestors even behind closed doors. I did not know, my husband, that history claimed so many men of action by the name of Liu. It pleased me to think thou mayest claim so long a lineage, as she went back to the dynasty of Ming and brought forth from his grave each poor man and woman and told us of— not his virtues. I should have been more indignant, perhaps, if I had not heard o'ermuch the wonders of thy family tree. I was impressed by the amount of knowledge acquired by the family of Li-ti. They must have searched the chronicles which evidently recorded only the unworthy acts of thy men-folk in the past. I hope that I will forget what I have heard, as some time when I am trying to escape from thine ancestors the tongue might become unruly.

At the end of three hours the woman was faint and very ill. I had one of the servants take her down to the boat, and sent a man home with her, bearing a letter saying she was sickening for home faces. She is old, and I did not want her to end her days in disgrace and shame.

But thine Honourable Mother! Thine Honourable Mother! Art thou not glad that thou art in a far-off country? She went from courtyard to courtyard, and for a time I fully expected she would send to the Yamen for the soldiers; then she realised the woman was within her right, and so restrained her-self. It nearly caused her death, as thou knowest thine Honourable Mother has not long practised the virtue of restraint, especially of the tongue. She was finally overcome taken to her chamber, and we brought her tea and heated wine, and tried in all our ways to make her forget the great humiliation. As she became no better, we sent for the man of medicine from the Eastern Gate, and he wished to burn her shoulders with a heated cash to remove the heat within her. To this she objected so strongly that he hastily gathered his utensils and departed looking fearfully over his shoulder from time to time as he passed quickly down the hillside.

Then I thought of her favourite priest from the monastery down below, and sent for him. He came with candle and incense and, I think, some rose wine for which the monastery is justly famous; and he chanted prayers, striking from time to time a little gong, until peace was restored and sleep came to her eyelids.

In the morning she wished to talk to Li-ti; but I feared for her, and I said, "You cannot speak of the ocean to a well-frog, nor sing of ice to a summer insect. She will not understand. She said Li-ti was without brains, a senseless thing of paint and powder. I said, "We will form her, we will make of her a wise woman in good time. She replied with bitterness, "Rotten wood cannot be carved nor walls of dirt be plastered." I could not answer, but I sent Li-ti to pass the day with Chih-peh at the Goldfish Temple, and when she returned the time was not so stormy.

All this made me unhappy, and the cares of this great household pressed heavily upon my shoulders. Please do not think the cares too heavy, nor that I do not crave the work. I know all labour is done for the sake of happiness, whether the happiness comes or no; and if I find not happiness, I find less time to dream and mourn and long for thee, my husband.

Thy Wife.

10

My Dear One,

We have been to a great festival at the Temple of the Goddess of a Thousand Hands. Thine Honourable Mother decided that we should go by boat part of the way, so the chairs were told to meet us at the Western Village Rest-house.

We hired from the city one of those great pleasure-boats, but it was not too great for us all. There was the August One, and four of her friends, then Li-ti, Mah-li and myself. We took the cook, the steward and three amahs, and it was indeed a time of feasting. It was the first time I had been upon the canal, and it was different from seeing it from the terrace. As we passed slowly along we could watch the life of the water people. On the banks were the great water-wheels turned by the village buffalo. In the deserted districts women were gathering reeds to make the sleeping mats and boat covers. The villages with their blue-grey houses and thatched roofs nestling among the groves of bamboos looked like chicklets sheltering under the outstretched wings of the mother hen.

We pushed our way through the crowded water-ways of the cities, where we could catch glimpses of the guests in the tea-houses or the keepers of the shops, or could watch the children leaning over the balconies. On the steps between the houses which led to the waterside women were washing clothes, or the dyers were cleansing the extra dye from the blue cotton which clothes all China's poor. We caught small bits of gossip and heard the laughter of all these people, who seemed happy at their work.

When we could again pass to the open canal we would watch the boats. I did not know there were so many boats in all the world. They floated slowly past us— big boats, little boats, those that went by sail, and those that went by oar. There were the boats of mandarins and merchants, those for passengers, and great unwieldy boats for rice. We saw the fishing-boats with their hungry, fierce-eyed cormorants sitting quietly in their places, waiting for the master to send them diving in the water for the fish they may not eat.

The canal was a great broad highway. Even the tow-paths had their patrons. Travellers on wheelbarrows, rich men in sedan-chairs, soldiers, coolies, chanting as they swung along with their burdens swinging from the bamboo on their shoulders, all going to or coming from the great city to which we drew nearer with each stroke.

At the rest-house the bearers were awaiting us, and we were carried up the long paved roadway to the temple. It seemed as if all the world had turned to praying— all the women world, that is. They were here, rich and poor, peasant and official's wife, but in the temple all of a sisterhood. We descended from our chairs in the courtyard and put our spirit money in the great burner, where it ascended in tiny flames side by side with that of the beggar woman, to the great God in the Heavens. We entered the temple, placed our candles, and lighted our incense. We made our obei-sance to the Many-handed Goddess and asked her blessing on our household for the year to come. Then I went to the Mother of Mercies, Kwan-yin, and made my deepest reverence, because for her my heart is full of love and gratitude. The other Gods I respect and make them all due worship, but, I feel they are far away from me. Kwan-yin, is the woman's God, and I feel her love for me. She shapes my way, and I know it is to her I owe it that my life flows on as a gentle stream, and I know that she cares for me and guards me now that thou art away and I have no one on whom to lean. When I go before her all fire of passion is extinguished in my heart, and my troubles and cares pass away and become small in the distance, even as the light of the morning stars pales and wanes at the coming of the sun. My heart is full of love for her, of a love that I cannot express. She has heard my prayers and answered them. She is my Kwan-yin, my Mother of Mercy, and each day I do some little deed for her, some little thing to show remembrance, so she will know the hours are not too full nor the days too short for me to place my offering on an altar built of love.

As we turned to leave the temple I glanced back at the great dark chamber and I saw the God of Light, the Buddha, sitting there so calm upon his throne, with the light of many candles before him and clouds of incense that floated to the roof. I thought, "He is all-powerful. I only prayed to him from out my lips, not with my heart. Perhaps—" So I returned. I prayed the mighty God with humble prayer to bring my loved one swiftly home to me; and then we left the temple. We walked slowly through the courtyards, looking at the great trees that stood like tall, grim sentinels guarding the place of prayer. Then we were taken by our bearers to the Goldfish Monastery in the hills. Dost thou remember it? Thou and I were there once in the springtime.

We bought the small round cakes from the priests and fed the greedy fish. They swarmed over the pool, pushing, nudging, fighting one another to get the morsels we threw them. Tiring of that, we had tea and sweetmeats served upon the terrace; then, after chatting for a time, we left for the boat. We drifted slowly homeward. Thy Mother and her friends discussed the earth, the moon, the sun and stars, as well as smaller matters, such as children, husbands, servants, schools— and upon the last thy Mother waxed most eloquent; as thou knowest, it is a sore subject with her, this matter of the new education. I heard her say: "All my sons have book knowledge. Of what use is it in the end? The cock crows and the dog barks. We know that, but the wisest of my sons cannot say why one crows and the other barks, nor why they crow or bark at all." Canst thou hear her, and see her shake her head dolefully over the dismal fact that thou hast left the narrow way of Confucius and the classics?

We came to the pathway just at sunset, and as I looked up at the old palace a little hurt came to my heart that thou wert not close by my side. It lay so peaceful there and quiet, the curving roofs like flights of doves who had settled down with their wings not yet quite folded. It brought remembrance that for me it was an empty palace. I will see no one— as Li-ti will— within the archway.

Thy Wife Who Loves Thee.

11

My Dear One,

Thy letter and the photographs received. Thou sayest it is a "flashlight" of a reception to thy Master, the Prince. I do not know exactly what that means, but there seem to be many people and—ladies. I have not shown thine Honourable Mother the picture, as she might ask thee to return at once. I do not criticise thy friends, nor could our Prince go to a place not fitting to his dignity, but—the ladies seem in my poor judgment most lightly clad.

The papers here are full of thy reception in that foreign land and of the honour that is paid the embassy. Thy brother read to all within the courtyard of the feasts that are given in honour of His Highness, and we were full proud, knowing well thou stoodst close by him at the time. Thy letters are a joy to me. We read them many times, and then I read those of Chih-peh, which talk of things I do not understand. Thou must not give the foolish boy ideas, as he prates most glibly of "republics" and "government of the people by the people," after he has received thy letters. That is for men of wisdom like thee, but not for foolish boys to carry with them to the tea-house.

Kwei-li.

12

My Dear One,

Thou askest me if I still care for thee, if the remembrance of thy face has grown less dear with the passing of the days. Dear one, thou knowest we Chinese women are not supposed to know of love, much less to speak of it. We read of it, we know it is the song of all the world, but it comes not to us unless by chance. We go to you as strangers, we have no choice, and if the Gods withhold their greatest gift, the gift of love, then life is grey and wan as the twilight of a hopeless day. Few women have the joy I feel when I look into my loved one's face and know that I am his and he is mine, and that our lives are twined together for all the days to come.

Do I love thee? I cannot tell. I think of thee by day and I dream of thee by night. I never want to hurt thee nor cause thee a moment's sorrow. I would fill my hands with happiness to lay down at thy feet. Thou art my life, my love, my all, and I am thine to hold through all the years.

13

My Dear One,

It is the time of school, and now all the day from the servants' courtyard I hear their droning voices chanting the sayings of Confucius. I did not know we had so many young lives within our compound until I saw them seated at their tables. I go at times and tell them tales which they much prefer to lessons, but of which thine Honourable Mother does not approve. I told them the other day of Pwan-ku. Dost thou remember him? How at the beginning of Time the great God Pwan-ku with hammer and chisel formed the earth. He toiled and he worked for eighteen thousand years, and each day increased in stature six feet, and, to give him room, the Heavens rose and the earth became larger and larger. When the Heavens were round and the earth all smooth, he died. His head became mountains, his breath the wind and the clouds, his voice the thunder. His arms and legs were the four poles, his veins the rivers, his muscles the hills and his flesh the fields. His eyes became the stars, his skin and hair the herbs and the trees, and the insects which touched him became people. Does not that make thee think of thy childhood's days?

They crowd around me and say, "Tell us more," just as I did with my old amah when she stilled me with the tales of the Gods. Yesterday, one small boy, the son of the chief steward, begged for a story of the sun. I had to tell him that my wisdom did not touch the sun, although I, in my foolish heart, think it a great God because it gives us warmth and we can feel its kindly rays. I said, "Thou hast seen the coolies tracking on the tow-path with their heavy wadded clothing wet with rain. If it were not for the kindly sun which dries them, how could they toil and work and drag the great rice-boats up to the water-gate? Is he not a God to them?"

I told them also of Chang-ngo, the great, great beauty who drank the cup of life eternal. She went to the moon, where the jealous Gods turned her into a great black toad. She is there, forever thinking, mourning over her lost beauty, and when we see the soft haze come over the face of the moon, we know that she is weeping and filling the space with her tears.

I perhaps am wrong to tell the foolish tales to the children, but they grow so tired of the hard benches and Chang-tai, the teacher, who glares at them so fiercely when they speak not quickly enough to please him.

There has been much gossip from the valley over the mountain-side. It seems an iron bridge is being put across the river, and strange men come and peer at the countryside through witch glasses. It has made the good spirits of the air to draw apart from the valley, and the cattle have died and the rice not ripened, and much sorrow has gone broadcast. The river overflowed, because they desecrated the Dragon's back by digging down into the earth that was sacred. I know nothing except what is brought from the market-place, and, as it does not concern us here on the mountain-side, I listen only with my ears, not with my mind.

The nights are long and cold. The moon casts silver shimmering lights over the valley below. We cannot stand long on the terrace but must stay close within our rooms near to the charcoal braziers. The wind sweeps o'er the rooftree with the wailing voice of a woman.

Oh, Soul of Mine, with weary heart the creeping days I'm counting.

Thy Wife.

14

My Dear One,

We have had a serious sickness come to all the countryside; rich and poor, peasant and merchant have suffered from a fever that will not abate. It raged for more than a moon before it was known the cause thereof. Dost thou remember the Kwan-lin Pagoda? Its ruin has long been a standing shame to the people of the province, and finally the Gods have resented their neglect and sent them this great illness. Over all the city the yellow edicts of the priests have been placed so as to meet the eye of all who travel. They are in the market-places, at the entrance of the tea-houses, standing on great boards at the doorways of the temples, in front of the water-gates, and at each city postern. They state that the Gods are angry and send to each man or household that will not give three days' work upon the Pagoda the fever that leaves him weak and ailing. They demand the labour of the city; and if it is not given freely, toil is sent the people in their sleep and they waken weary, and must so remain until the work is finished.

We did not hearken to the summons until Chih-peh, thy brother, fell ill with the sickness. He grew worse each day, until Li-ti and thine Honourable Mother were panic-stricken. At last the chairs were ordered, and thy Mother and I went to the monastery on the hillside to consult with the old abbot, who is most full of wisdom. Thine Honourable Mother told him of the illness which had assailed her son, and begged him to tell her if it were the illness of the Pagoda. He meditated long and seriously, then he said, "My daughter, the Gods are no respecter of persons; they wish the service of your son." "But," thine Honourable Mother objected, "he is no workman. He cannot labour upon the Pagoda." The abbot said, "There are more ways of giving service than the labour of the hands. The Gods will allow him to contribute of his wealth and buy the toil of other men, and thus he may cancel his obligation." The August One satisfied the greedy heart of the priest, and then he told her to go and make her beisance to the God of Light, the great Buddha, and see what message he had for her.

She took the hollow bamboo filled with the numbered slices

of wood and, prostrating herself three times before the Great One, shook it slowly until one detached itself from its brothers and fell to the floor. The abbot then handed her a slip of paper which read:

"Wisdom sits by the Western Gate And gives health and happiness to those who wait."

These words meant nothing to thine Honourable Mother; and after giving the abbot more silver, he said, "Beside the Western Gate sits the owl of wisdom, the great doctor Chow-fong. His father and his father's father were wise; their study was mankind, and to him has come all their stores of knowledge. He has books of wonderful age, that tell him the secret of the world. Go to him; he will give you the plan of healing."

We started for the Western Gate, and I, in my wicked heart, spoke thoughts that should have been closely locked within my breast. I said, "Perhaps the doctor and the priest have formed a combination most profitable to the two. If we had gone to the doctor first, we might have been sent to the abbot." It was a great mistake to mention such a dreadful thing, and I realised it instantly; as thou knowest, the Elder One has a tongue of eloquence, and I was indeed glad that her bearers carried her at least ten paces from my bearers— and the way was long.

Even thine Honourable Mother was awed at the solemn looks of this great man of medicine who, in his dim room with dried bats hanging from the ceiling beams and a dragon's egg close by his hand, glared at her through his great goggles like a wise old owl. She apologised for disturbing so great a man at his studies, but she was the bearer of a message from the abbot. He read it carefully, then took down a monstrous book entitled "The Golden Mirror of Medical Practice," and solemnly pored over its pages. At last he wrote upon a paper, then chanted:

"In a building tall, by the city wall, In the street of the Tower of Gold, Is the plant of health, long life and wealth, In the claws of the Dragon bold."

The August One took the paper, laid some silver upon the table, and we hurried from his doorway, glad to be free from his fearful presence. When we entered the chairs and looked to the paper for directions to give the bearers, the characters were meaningless to us. I repeated his chant, and the head bearer said, "There is a shop of drugs in the street of the Tower of Gold, and the sign of the place is a Golden Dragon's Claw."

We soon were there, and waited in our chairs while the bearer took the paper into the maker of medicines. We waited long, and thine Honourable Mother would have been impatient if sleep had not kindly made her forget the waiting hours. I, sitting in my chair, could look through the archways into the big covered courtyards where blind men were grinding herbs. They were harnessed to great stones, and went round and round all day, like buffalo at the water-wheel. I wondered why the Gods had put them at this service. What sins they had committed in their other life, to be compelled to work like beasts, grinding the herbs that would bring health and life to others, while they lived on in darkness. Often I would hear the soft call of the deer as they moved restlessly in their tiny cells. I know their horns, when powdered fine with beetles' wings, is the cure for fevers and all ailments of the blood, but why could not the wise ones of the earth have found some herb or weed to take their place and give these wild ones of the woods their freedom? Finally, the bearer came with a tiny jar, too small, it seemed, to take such time in mixing, and we returned to the waiting Li-ti.

The medicine was black and nasty and smelled not sweetly, which proved its strength. Chih-peh got slowly better, and the world again looked fair to Li-ti, and the song came to her lips. The flowers were put in the hair, the gay dresses were brought out of their boxes, and she was, as of old, our butterfly.

We laughed at her for her fright, but I thought, if it had been thou who wast ill, and I did not know the cure! Oh, dear one, dost thou understand that, to a woman who loves, her husband is more than Heaven, more than herself? All that she is not, all that she lacks, all that she desires to be, is her beloved. His breath alone can bring peace to her heart, and it is he alone who teaches her the depth of passionate joy there is in love and life and all things beautiful.

I am, thy wife.

15

My Dear One,

Thine Honourable Mother is beset by the desire or marrying. No, do not start; it is not or herself she is thinking. She will go to the River or Souls mourning thine Honourable Father, and a pailo will be erected in her honour. It is or her household she is thinking. She says our rooftree is too small to shelter four women, three or whom have little brains— and that includes thy humble, loving wire— but why she should wish to exchange Mah-li, whom she knows, for a strange woman whom she does not know, passes my understanding. She seems not overfond of daughters-in-law, if one judge from chance remarks.

First, before I speak or Mah-li, I must tell thee of thy brother. Thine Honourable Mother is right— it were better that he marry and have a heel rope that leads him homewards. He is unruly and passes overmuch time at the Golden Lotus Tea-house. He is not bad or wicked. He lives but for the moment, and the moment is often wine-flushed. He will not work or study, and many times at night I send away the gatekeeper and leave my amah at the outer archway, so thy Mother will not know the hour he enters. He is young, and has chosen friends not equal to himself, and they have set his feet in the path-way that slopes downward.

He does not wish to marry. We have told him that marriage is a will of the Gods and must be obeyed. "Man does not attain by himself, nor, Woman by herself, but like the one-winged birds of our childhood's tale, they must rise together." It is useless to talk to him. A spark of fire will not kindle wood that is still too green, and I rear he is in love with life, and youth, and freedom.

I do not wish to doubt the wisdom of the August One, but I think she made a mistake in her choice of a bride for Chih-mo. She chose Tai-lo, the daughter of the Prefect of Chih-Ii. The arrangements were nearly made, the dowry even was discussed, but when the astrologer cast their horoscopes to see if they could pass their life in peace together, it was found that the ruler of Chih-mo's life was a lion, and that of the bride's, a swallow, so it was clearly seen they could not share one rooftree. I fear (I would not have this come to the ears of thine Honourable Mother) that some silver was left upon the doorstep of the astrologer. Chih-mo asked of me the loan of an hundred taels, and I saw the wife of the reader of the stars pass by with a new gown of red and gold brocade.

I think Chih-mo had seen Tai-lo. Report gives her small beauty. Yet, as the Elder One says, "Musk is known by its perfume, and not by the druggist's label." Quite likely she would have made a good wife; and— we have one beauty in the household— it is enough.

There is much wailing in the courtyards. The gardener and the bearer and the watchman are having bound the feet of their small daughters. The saying, "For every pair of golden lillies' there is a kang of tears," is true. I am so sorry for them. Just when they want to run and play, they must sit all day with aching feet. My amah wished to put on the heavy bindings, but I would not permit it. I said, "Do you want little eyes to fill with tears each time they see you coming across the courtyard? If their grandmothers do not come, let some old women from the village do the cruel thing."

The happy rains of the spring are here. It is not the cold, drear rain of autumn, but dancing, laughing rain that comes sweeping across the valley, touching the rice-fields lovingly, and bringing forth the young green leaves of the mulberry. I hear it patter upon the roof at night-time, and in the morning all the earth seems cleansed and new; fresh colours greet mine eye when I throw back my casement.

When wilt thou come to me, thou keeper of my heart?

Thy Wife.

16

Dear One,

"He whose faults are never told him Doubtless deems the angels mould him."

That cannot be said of three women of thy household.

It is Mah-li this time on whom the wrath descends. She and Li-ti were broidering in the western room, where they could get the last rays of the sun. Perhaps they were speaking on forbidden subjects— I do not know; but thine Honourable Mother entered quietly and reproved them, and (even when I write it I blush for her) Mah-li said to her Honourable Mother, "Only cats and cranes and thieves walk silently." Thy Mother was speechless with anger, and justly so, and now it is decided that Mah-li must be married. She needs a stronger hand than a woman's. Is it not ridiculous, little Mah-li needing a strong hand?

At first the August One considered Meng-wheh, the prefect at Sung-dong. He is old and cross, but when I remonstrated, I was told that he was rich. His many tens of thousands of sycee are supposed to weigh more than youth and love. I said, "Though he bar with gold his silver door," a man cannot keep the wife who loves him not. Thine Honourable Mother thought more wisely, and after days of consideration entered into consultation with the family of Sheng Ta-jen in regard to his son. It seems Mah-li is doomed to marriage soon, and she does not know whether she is happy or sorrowful. She is turned this way and that, as the seed of the cotton-tree is swayed by the coming and going of the wind. Today she laughs, tomorrow she weeps. Thy Mother has lost all patience with her, and, as she always does when her own words rail her, I heard her quoting the Sage: "Just as ducks' legs though short cannot be lengthened without pain, nor cranes' legs though long be shortened without misery to the crane, neither can sense be added to a silly woman's head."

I feel that thine Honourable Mother is unkind to Mah-li. She is a flower, a flower that has her place in life the same as the morning-glory, which is loved just as fondly by the Gods as the pine-tree which stands so stately upon the hillside. She is light and pure and dainty as the fragrance of perfumed air, and I do not want to see her go to a family who will not understand her youth and love of play.

Mah-li has asked of me money, and with it bought a great candle for each day, which she sends down the mountain-side to be placed before Kwan-yin. I asked her to tell me her prayer, that needed so large an offering. The unfilial girl said she prayed, "Kwan-yin, send me a husband with no family."

Such a lot of petty gossip I pour into thine ears, yet thou wouldst know the happenings of thine household. Of the world outside, thy brother writes thee. My world is here within these walls.

Thy Wife.

17

My Dear One,

Thine house of intrigue. Deep, dark intrigue and plotting. Thy wife has lent herself to a most unwomanly thing, and doubtless thou wilt tell her so, but Mah-li begged so prettily, I could refuse her nothing. I told thee in my last letter that thine Honourable Mother had been regarding the family of Sheng Ta-jen with a view to his son as husband of Mah-li. It is settled, and Mah-li leaves us in the autumn. None of us except Chih-peh has seen the young man, and Mah-li did a most immodest thing the other day. She came to me and asked me to find out from Chih-peh if he were handsome, if he were young— all the questions that burn the tongue of a young girl, but which she must keep within tightly closed lips if she would not be thought unmaidenly. I asked thy brother; but his answer was not in regard to the questions Mah-li wished so much to know. So we arranged a plan— a plan that caused me many nights of sleeplessness. It was carried out and— still the sky is blue, the stars are bright at night, and the moon shines just as softly on the valley.

The first part of the plan was for Li-ti. She must persuade Chih-peh to ask Shen-go to spend the day with him at the Fir-tree Monastery. When he knew the meaning of the invitation he refused. He was shocked, and properly; as it was a thing unheard-of. He could not understand why Mah-li would not be content with her mother's choice. Li-ti brought all her little ways to bear— and Chih-peh can refuse her nothing. At the Feast of the Moon thy brother asked three friends to join him at the monastery and stroll amongst its groves.

The rest of the plan was for me to carry out; and I, thy wife, displayed a talent for diplomacy. I noticed that the cheeks of our Honourable Mother were pale, that she seemed listless, that her step was wearied. I said doubtless she was tired of being shut within the compound walls with three aimless, foolish women, and proposed a feast or pilgrimage. I mentioned the Goldfish Pond, knowing she was tired of it; spoke of the Pagoda on the Hills, knowing full well that she did not like the priests therein;

then, by chance, read from a book the story of the two kings. It is the tale of the King of Hangchow and the King of Soochow who, in the olden time, divided our great valley between them. The King of Hangchow was an old man and the cares of state fell heavily upon his shoulders. The King of Soochow was a man, eaten up with mad ambitions. He began to tread upon the lands of the old King, taking now a farmhouse, now a village, and at last a city, until the poor old King was threatened at his very gateway by the army of the young man. The young King had strength, but the old King had guile, so he made a peace with his enemy for one year. He sent him presents, costly silks and teas, and pearls and jade and ginseng, and, last and best, a beautiful slave-girl, the most beautiful in the province. The young King was delighted, and forgot his warring, passing all his days within the women's quarters.

As the winter waned and the spring came, the slave-girl sickened, said she panted for the hillsides, and she pointed to the mountain outside his city walls. He was a foolish King, and he builded for her a palace, and she moved there with her women. The King was lonely in the city, and he passed his days with the women in the palace on the mountain. While living there in pleasure, and his army in the city, the old King of Hangchow sent his soldiers; and soon there was no King of Soochow, only a slave-girl decked with many jewels was taken back with honour to the old King's city.

I read all this to thine Honourable Mother, and told her we could see the ruins of the fish-pond, of the palace, see the fallen marbles from the tea-house, and— the chairs were ordered, and we went. We wandered over deserted pathways, saw the lotus pools once filled with goldfish, picked our way through lonely courtyards, climbed the sunken steps of terraces that had once been gay with flowers. It all was melancholy, this palace built for pleasure, now a mass of crumbling ruins, and it saddened us. We sat upon the King's bench that overlooked the plain, and from it I pointed out the Fir-tree Monastery in the distance. I spoke of their famous tea, sun-dried with the flowers of jessamine, and said it might bring cheer and take away the gloom caused by the sight of death and vanished grandeurs now around us.

We were carried swiftly along the pathways that wound in and out past farm villages and rest-houses until we came to the monastery, which is like a yellow jewel in its setting of green fir-trees. The priests made us most welcome, and we drank of their tea, which has not been overpraised, sitting at a great open window looking down upon the valley. Strolling in the courtyard was Chih-peh with his three friends. Mah-li never raised her eyes; she sat as maidens sit in public, but— she saw.

We came home another pathway, to pass the resting-place of Sheng-dong, the man who at the time of famine fed the poor and gave his all to help the needy. The Gods so loved him that when his body was carried along the road-way to the Resting-place of his Ancestors, all the stones stood up to pay him reverence. One can see them now, standing straight and stiff, as if waiting for his command to lie down again.

Art thou dissatisfied with me? Have I done wrong? Dear One, it means so much to Mah-li. Let her dream these months of waiting. It is hard to keep wondering, doubting, fearing one knows not what, hoping as young girls hope. But now she has seen him. To me he was just a straight-limbed, bright-faced boy; to her he is a God. There are no teeth so white, no hair so black, and man were not born who walked with such a noble stride. It will make the summer pass more quickly, and the thought of the marriage-chair will not be to her the gateway of a prison.

Art thou not tired of that far-off country? Each time I break the seal of thy dear letter I say, "Perhaps this time— it holds for me my happiness. It will say, 'I am coming home to thee'." I am longing for that message.

Thy Wife.

18

My Dear One,

It will soon be the Feast of the Springtime. Even now the roads are covered with the women coming to the temple carrying their baskets of spirit money and candles to lay before the Buddha.

Spring will soon be truly here; the buds are everywhere. Everything laughs from the sheer joy of laughter. The sun looks down upon the water in the canal and it breaks into a thousand little ripples from pure gladness. I too am happy, and I want to give of my happiness. I have put a great kang of tea down by the rest-house on the tow-path, so that they who thirst may drink. Each morning I send Chang-tai, the gate-keeper, down to the man who lives in the little reed hut he has builded by the grave of his father. For three years he will live there, to show to the world his sorrow. I think it very worthy and filial of him, so I send him rice each morning. I have also done another thing to express the joy that is deep within my heart. The old abbot, out of thankfulness that the tall poles were not erected before the monastery gateway, has turned the fields back of the temple into a freeing-place for animals. There one may acquire merit by buying a sheep, a horse, a dog, a bird, or a snake that is to be killed, and turning it loose where it may live and die a natural death, as the Gods intended from the beginning. I have given him a sum of money, large in his eyes but small when compared to my happiness, to aid him in this worthy work. I go over in the morning and look at the poor horses and the dogs, and wonder whose soul is regarding me from out of their tired eyes.

Let me hear that thou art coming, man of mine, and I will gather dewdrops from the cherry-trees and bathe me in their perfume to give me beauty that will hold thee close to me.

I am, Thy Wife.

19

My Dear One

, I have received thy letter telling me thou wilt not be here until the summer comes. Then, I must tell thee my news, as the springtime is here, the flowers are budding, the grass is green, soon the plum-tree in the courtyard will be white. I am jealous of this paper that will see the delight and joy in thine eyes. In the evening I watch the rice boats pass along the canal, where the water is green and silvery like the new leaves of the willow, and I say, "Perhaps when you return, I shall be the mother of a child." Ah—! I have told thee. Does it bring thee happiness, my lord? Does it make a quick little catch in thy breath? Does thy pulse quicken at the thought that soon thou wilt be a father?

Thou wilt never know what this has meant to me. It has made the creature live that was within my soul, and my whole being is bathed with its glory. Thou wilt never know how many times I have gone down the pathway to the temple and asked this great boon of our Lady of Mercy. She granted it, and my life is made perfect. I am indeed a woman, fulfilling a woman's destiny. If a woman bear not sons for her lord, what worth her life? Do we not know that the first of the seven causes for putting away a wife is that she brings no sons into the world to worship at the graves of her husband's ancestors? But I, Kwei-li, that will not be said of me.

Sometimes I think, "If something should happen; if the Gods should be jealous of my happiness and I should not see thee more?" Then the heart of the woman throbs with fear, and I throw myself at the feet of Kwan-yin and beg for strength. She gives me peace and brings to my remembrance that the bond of fate is sealed within the moon. There is no place for fear, for aught but love; my heart is filled so with its happiness.

Thy Wife.

20

My Dear One,

The spring has come, and with it some new pulse of life beats through my quiet veins. I spend long hours upon the terrace, breathing in the perfume of the many flowers. The cherry-blossoms are a glory. The whole steep hillside is covered with a fairy lace, as if some God knew how we hungered after beauty and gave us these pink blossoms to help us to forget the bare cold earth of winter.

It is the time of praying, and all the women with their candles and their incense are bending knees and chanting prayers to Kwan-yin for the blessing of a son. There is a pilgrimage to the Kwem-li Pagoda. I can see it in the distance, with its lotus bells that sway and ring with each light breath of wind. One does not think of it as a thing of brick and mortar, or as a many-storied temple, but as a casket whose jewels are the prayers of waiting, hoping women.

You ask me how I pass my days? I cannot tell. At dawn, I wake with hope and listen to the song of the meadow-lark. At noon, I dream of my great happiness to come. At sunset, I am swept away into the land of my golden dreams, into the heart of my golden world that is peopled with but three— Thou, Him, and Me. I am drifting happily, sleepily, forgetting care, waiting for the Gods to bring my joy.

Thy Wife.

21

My Dear One,

My courtyard is filled with the sounds of chatting women. I have sent for the sewiing-women and those who do embroidery, and the days are passed in making little garments. We are all so busy; Li-ti, Mah-li, even thine Honourable Mother takes again the needle and shows us how she broidered jackets for thee when thou wert young. The piles of clothing grow each day, and I touch them and caress them and imagine I can see them folding close a tiny form. There are jackets, trousers, shoes, tiny caps and thick warm blankets.

I send for Blind Chun, the story-teller, and he makes the hours pass quickly with his tales of by-gone days. The singers and the fortune-tellers all have found the path that leads up to our gateway, knowing they will find a welcome.

I am, Thy Happy Wife.

22

I send thee cherry-blossoms. They grew within thy courtyard, and each tiny petal will bring to thee remembrance of thy wife who loves thee well.

23

If thou couldst see my courtyard! It seems carpeted with snow, so many are the cherry-blossoms on its pavement. They say I am untidy that I permit it to be untouched by broom or brush. It is cleaned and spotless all the year, save at this the time of cherry-blossoms, when 'tis untrodden and unswept.

I cannot write thee merely household cares and gossip. I am so filled with happiness, I can only dream and wonder. Joy is beating with his wings just outside my open window, and soon all the gates of Heaven will be opened wide to me.

Thy Wife.

24

He is here, beloved, thy son! I put out my hand and touch him, and the breath of the wind through the pine-trees brings the music of the Gods to me. He is big and strong and beautiful. I see in his eyes as in a mirror the reflection of thy dear face, and I know he is thine and mine, and we three are one. He is my joy, my son, my first-born. I am tired, my lord, the brush is heavy, but it is such a happy, happy tired.

Thy Wife.

25

Is there anything so wonderful as being the mother of a son? I simply sing, and laugh, and live— oh, how I live the long days through. I have happiness enough for all the world, and I want to give and give and give. Thy mother says that all the beggers within the province know there is rice outside our gateway; but when I look into my son's eyes, and feel his tiny fingers groping in my neck, I feel I must give of my plenty to those who have no joy.

Oh, husband mine, come back and see thy son!

26

Dost thou know what love is? Thou canst not till thou holdest Love itself within thy very arms. I thought I loved thee. I smile now at the remembrance of that feeble flickering flame that was as like unto the real love as the faint, cold beam of the candle is to the rays of the glorious sun. Now— now— thou art the father of my son. Thou hast a new place in my heart. The tie that binds our hearts together is stronger than a rope of twisted bamboo, it is a bond, a love bond, that never can be severed. I am the mother of thy first-born— thou hast given me my man-child. Love thee— love thee—! Now I know!

I am Thine Own.

27

I am wroth with thy brother Chih-peh. He is a man of very small discernment. He does not see the wonders of thy son. He says he cannot see that he is a child of more than mortal beauty. I sorrow for him. The Gods have surely drawn a film before his eyes.

But I cannot bear resentment, there is no room in me for aught but love and the days are far too short to hold my happiness. I pass them near my baby. I croon to him sweet lullabies at which the others laugh. I say, "Thou dost not understand? Of course not, 'tis the language of the Gods," and as he sleeps I watch his small face grow each day more like to thine. I give long hours to thinking of his future. He must be a man like thee, strong, noble, kindly, bearing thy great name with honour, so that in years to come it will be said, "The first-born son of Kwei-li was a great and worthy man."

At night I lie beside him and am jealous of the sleep that takes him from my sight. The morning comes and sets my heart to beating at the thought that one more long, sweet day has come to me in which to guard, and love, and cherish him.

Thy Happy Wife.

28

It has been a wonderful day. Thy son has had his first reception. It is just one moon ago since I found him lying by my side,
and now we have had the feast of the shaving of the head. All our
friends came, and they brought him beautiful presents. Chih-lo
gave a cap with all the Gods upon the front and long red tassels to
hang down by each ear. Li-ti gave him shoes that she herself had
broidered, with a cat's face on the toes and the ears and whiskers
outstanding. They will make him careful or his steps and sure-
footed as the cat. Mah-li gave him a most wonderful silver box to
hang around his neck and in which I will keep his amulets. There
were many things which I will not take the time to tell thee. I am
sorry to say that thy son behaved himself unseemly. He screamed
and kicked as the barber shaved his tiny head. I was much dis-
tressed, but they tell me it is a sign that he will grow to be a valiant
man.

I gave a feast, and such a feast! It will be remembered for many
moons. Even thine Honourable Mother said I showed the knowledge of what was due my guests upon so great an occasion. We
also gave to him his milk name. It is Ten Thousand Springtimes, as
he came at blossom-time; but I call him that only within my heart,
as I do not wish the jealous Gods to hear. Then I speak of him,
I say "The Stupid One," "The Late-Born," so they will think I
do not care for him and will not covet me my treasure.

I am tired; it has been a happy day. The Gods are good to,
Kwei-li.

29

My Dear One, Another marriage within our compound. Dost thou remember the servant Cho-to, who came to us soon after I became thy bride? She will soon marry a man in the village of Soong-tong, and she is very happy. She has not seen him, of course, but her mother says he is good and honest and will make for her a suitable husband. I talked to her quite seriously, as my age and many moons of marriage allow me. I told her that only by practising modesty, humility and gentleness could she walk safely on the path that leads to being the mother of sons.

To be the mother of sons is not always a happiness. Ling-ti, the shoemaker, was here this morning, and he was in great distress. His baby, three months old, died with a fever and he had no money to pay for burial. This morning he arose early, before the mother awakened, and took it to the baby tower outside the city. It is lying in there now, with all the other little children whose parents were too poor to give them proper burial. It made a quick, sad hurt within me, and I went quickly to find my baby. Thou wilt not laugh, but I have pierced his right ear and put a ring therein, so the Gods will think he is a girl and not desire him.

I hear thy son.

Thy Wife.

30

My Dear One,

There has been great talk of evil eyes. Not that I believe the servants' tales; but— thine Honourable Mother, Li-ti, and thy wife have been to the Holy Man who dwells underneath the Great Magnolia-tree near the street of the Leaning Willow. He lives alone within a little house of matting, and has acquired great merit by his virtuous acts. He wears around his unbound hair a band of metal that is the outward sign of his great holiness. He lives alone in peace and with untroubled mind. In his great wisdom he has learned that peace is the end and aim of life; not triumph, success, nor riches, but that the greatest gift from all the Gods is peace. I purchased from him an amulet for my "Stupid One," my treasure, as some one might come within our courtyard and cast his eye upon our child with bad intent.

Come to me, my husband. Tell me thou art coming. Thou wilt find me standing in the outer archway with thy son within mine arms. I long for thee.

Thy Wife.

31

My days are filled with happiness. I go out on the terrace and look far down the hillside that is covered with azaleas, pink and orange and mauve. I hold my son and say, "Look, thy father will come to us from the city yonder. Our eyes of love will see him from far away, there by the willow-pattern tea-house. He will come nearer— nearer— and we will not hear the beat of his bearers' feet upon the pathway because of the beating of our hearts." He smiles at me, he understands. He is so wonderful, thy son. I would "string the sunbeams for his necklace or draw down the moon with cords to canopy his bed."

Come back and see thy son.

Kwei-li.

32

My Dear One,

Thy letter has come saying thou wilt be here soon. It came on the day I went to the temple to make my offering of thanks for the gift of our son.

I put on my richest gown, the blue one with the broidery of gold. I dressed my hair with jessamine flowers, and wore all the jewels thou hast given me. My boy was in his jacket of red, his trousers of mauve, his shoes of purple, and his cap with the many Gods. When I was seated in the chair he was placed in my lap, and a man was sent ahead with cash to give the beggars, because I wished all the world to be happy on this my day of rejoicing.

My bearers carried me to the very steps of the throne on which Kwan-yin was seated. I made my obeisance, I lighted the large red candles and placed them before the Goddess of Heaven. Then I took our son before the Buddha, the Name, the Lord of Light, the All-Powerful, and touched his head three times to the mat, to show that he would be a faithful follower and learn to keep the law.

We went home by the valley road, and my heart kept beating in tune to the pat-pat of the bearers' feet on the pathway. It was all so beautiful. The trailing vines on the mountain-side, the ferns in the cool dark places, the rich green leaves of the mulberry-trees, the farmers in the paddy fields, all seemed filled with the joy of life. And I, Kwei-li, going along in my chair with my son on my knee, was the happiest of them all. The Gods have given me everything; they have nothing more to bestow. I am glad I have gone to the mountain-side each day to thank them for their gifts.

The Gods are good, my loved one, they are good to thy, Kwei-li.

33

I am alone on the mountain-top. I have gone the pathway the last time to lay my offering at the feet of Kwan-yin. She does not hear my voice. There is no Goddess of Mercy. She is a thing of gold and wood, and she has mocked my despair, has laughed at the heart that is within me, that is alive and full of an anguish such as she has never known.

My son, my man-child is dead. The life has gone from his body, the breath from his lips. I have held him all the night close to my heart and it does not give him warmth. They have taken him from me and told me he has gone to the Gods. There are no Gods. There are no Gods. I am alone.

34

He had thine eyes— he was like to thee. Thou wilt never know thy son and mine, my Springtime. Why could they not have left thy son for thee to see? He was so strong and beautiful, my first-born.

35

Do not chide me. I cannot write. What do I do? I do not know. I lie long hours and watch the tiny mites that live within the sun's bright golden rays, and say, "Why could I not exchange my womanhood, that hopes and loves and sorrows, for one of those small dancing spots within the sunbeams? At least they do not feel."

At night sleep does not touch my eyelids. I lie upon the terrace. I will not go within my chamber, where 'tis gloom and darkness. I watch the stars, a silver, mocking throng, that twinkle at me coldly, and then I see the moon mount slowly her pathway of the skies. The noises of the night come to me softly, as if they knew my sorrow, and the croaking frogs and the crickets that find lodging by the lotus pool seem to feel with me my loneliness, so plaintive is their cry.

I feel the dawn will never come, as if 'twere dead or slumbered; but when at last he comes, I watch him touch the hillside, trees, and temples with soft grey fingers, and bring to me a beauty one does not see by day. The night winds pass with sighs among the pine-trees, and in passing give a loving touch to bells upon pagodas that bring their music faint to me. The dawn is not the golden door of happiness. It only means another day has come and I must smile and talk and live as if my heart were here.

Oh, man of mine, if but thy dream touch would come and bid me slumber, I would obey.

Thy Wife.

36

They have put a baby in my arms, a child found on the tow-path, a beggar child. I felt I could not place another head where our dear boy had lain, and I sat stiff and still, and tried to push away the little body pressing close against me; but at touch of baby mouth and fingers, springs that were dead seemed stirring in my heart again. At last I could not bear it, and I leaned my face against her head and crooned His lullaby:

"The Gods on the rooftree guard pigeons from harm And my little pigeon is safe in my arms."

I cannot tell thee more. My heart is breaking.

37

I have given to this stranger-child, this child left to die upon the tow-path, the clothes that were our son's. She was cold, and thy Mother came to me so gently and said, "Kwei-li, hast thou no clothing for the child that was found by thy servants?" I saw her meaning, and I said, "Would'st thou have me put the clothing over which I have wept, and that is now carefully laid away in the camphor-wood box, upon this child?" She said— and thou would'st not know thy Mother's voice, her bitter words are only as the rough shell of the lichee nut that covers the sweet meat hidden within— she said, "Why not, dear one? This one needs them, and the hours thou passest with them are only filled with saddened memories." I said to her, "This is a girl, a beggar child. I will not give to her the clothing of my son. Each time I looked upon her it would be a knife plunged in my heart." She said to me, "Kwei-li, thou art not a child, thou art a woman. Of what worth that clothing lying in that box of camphor-wood? Does it bring back thy son? Some day thou wilt open it, and there will be nothing but dust which will reproach thee. Get them and give them to this child which has come to us out of the night."

I went to the box and opened it, and they lay there, the little things that had touched his tiny body. I gave them, the trousers of purple, the jackets of red, the embroidered shoes, the caps with the many Buddhas. I gave them all to the begger child.

I am, Thy Wife.

38

I am reproached because I will not go to the temple. It is filled with the sounds of chanting which comes to me faintly as I lie upon the terrace. There are women there, happy women, with their babies in their arms, while mine are empty. There are others there in sorrow, laying their offerings at the feet of Kwan-yin. They do not know that she does not feel, nor care, for woman-kind. She sits upon her lotus throne and laughs at mothers in despair. How can she feel, how can she know, that thing of gilded wood and plaster?

I stay upon my terrace, I live alone within my court of silent dreams. For me there are no Gods.

39

They have brought to me from the market-place a book of a new God. I would not read it. I said, "There are too many Gods—why add a new one? I have no candles or incense to lay before an image." But— I read and saw within its pages that He gave rest and love and peace. Peace— what the holy man desired, the end of all things— peace. And I, I do not want to lose the gift of memory; I want remembrance, but I want it without pain.

The cherry-blossoms have bloomed and passed away. They lingered but a moment's space, and, like my dream of spring, they died. But, passing, they have left behind the knowledge that we'll see them once again. There must be something, somewhere, to speak to despairing mothers and say, "Weep not! You will see your own again."

I do not want a God of temples. I have cried my prayers to Kwan-yin, and they have come back to me like echoes from a deadened wall. I want a God to come to me at night-time, when I am lying lonely, wide-eyed, staring into darkness, with all my body aching for the touch of tiny hands. I want that God who says, "I give thee Peace," to stand close by my pillow and touch my wearied eyelids and bring me rest.

I have been dead— enclosed within a tomb of sorrow and despair; but now, at words but dimly understood, a faint new life seems stirring deep within me. A Voice speaks to me from out these pages, a Voice that says, "Come unto Me all ye weary and heavy-laden, and I will give thee rest." My longing soul cries out, "Oh, great and unknown God, give me this rest!" I am alone, a woman, helpless, stretching out my arms in darkness, but into my world of gloom has come a faint dim star, a star of hope that says to me, "There is a God."

Part 2

PREFACE

These letters were written by Kwei-li twenty-five years after those written to her husband when she was a young girl of eighteen. They are, therefore, the letters of the present-day Chinese woman of the old school, a woman who had by education and environment exceptional opportunities to learn of the modern world, but who, like every Eastern woman, clings with almost desperate tenacity to the traditions and customs of her race. Indeed, however the youth of Oriental countries may be changing, their mothers always exhibit that characteristic of woman-hood, conservatism, which is to them the safe-guard of their homes. Unlike the Western woman, accustomed to a broader horizon, the woman of China, secluded for generations within her narrow courtyards, prefers the ways and manners which she knows, rather than flying to ills she knows not of. It is this self-protective instinct that makes the Eastern woman the foe to those innovations which are slowly but surely changing the face of the entire Eastern, yard.

The former letters were written out of the quiet, domestic scenes of the primitive, old China, while the present letters come out of the confused revolutionary atmosphere of the new China. Kwei-li's patriotism and hatred of the foreigner grows out of the fact that, as wife of the governor of one of the chief provinces, she had been from the beginning en rapport with the intrigues, the gossip, and the rumours of a revolution which, for intricacy of plot and hidden motive, is incomparable with any previous national change on record. Her attitude toward education as seen in her relationship with her son educated in England and America reveals the attitude of the average Chinese father and mother if they would allow their inner feelings to speak.

Kwei-li's religion likewise exhibits the tendency of religious attitude on the part of the real Chinese, especially those of the older generation. It is touched here and there by the vital spark of Christianity, but at the centre continues to be Chinese and inseparably associated with the worship of ancestors and the reverence for those gods whose influence has been woven into the early years of impressionable life.

That the hope of the educational, social, and religious change in China rests with the new generation is evident to all. The Chinese father and mother will sail in the wooden ships which their sons and daughters are beginning to leave for barks of steel.

There is little doubt that new China will be Westernised in every department of her being. No friend of China hopes for such sudden changes, however, as will prevent the Chinese themselves from permeating the new with their own distinctive individuality. There is a charm about old China that only those who have lived there can understand, and there is a charm about these dainty ladies, secluded within their walls, which the modern woman may lose in a too sudden transition into the air of the Western day.

Let Europe, let America, let the West come to China, but let the day be far distant when we shall find no longer in the women's courtyards such mothers as Kwei-li.

1

My Dear Mother,

Thy son has received his appointment as governor of this province, and we are at last settled in this new and strange abode. We are most proud of the words pronounced by His Excellency Yuan when giving him his power of office. He said:

"You, Liu, are an example of that higher patriotism rarely met with in official life, which recognises its duty to its Government, a duty too often forgotten by the members of a great family such as that of which you are the honoured head, in the obligation to the Clan and the desire to use power for personal advantage. Your official record has been without stain; and especially your work among the foreigners dwelling in our land has been accomplished with tact and discretion. I am sending you to Shanghai, which is the most difficult post in the Republic because of its involved affairs with the foreign nations, knowing that the interests of the Republic will be always safe in your hands."

I write thee this because I know thy mother-heart will rejoice that our President shows such confidence in thy son, and that his many years of service to his country have been appreciated.

Shanghai truly is a difficult place at present. There are fifteen nationalities here represented by their consuls, and they are all watching China and each other with jealous eyes, each nation fearing that another will obtain some slight advantage in the present unsettled state of our country. The town is filled with adventurers, both European and Chinese, who are waiting anxiously to see what attitude the new Governor takes in regard to the many projects in which they are interested. My husband says nothing and allows them to wonder. It is better for them, because, like all schemers, if they had nothing to give them anxious nights and troubled dreams, they would not be happy.

We found the Yamen not suitable for our large household, as it did not lend itself readily to the reception of foreigners and the innovations and new customs that seem to be necessary for the fulfillment of the duties of a Chinese official under this new order. As thy son was selected governor of this province because of his knowledge of foreign lands and customs, it is necessary for him to live, partly at least, the life of a European; but let me assure thee that, so far as I am concerned, and so far as I can influence it, our life behind the screens will always be purely Chinese, and the old, unchanged customs that I love will rule my household. I will surrender no more than is necessary to this new tide of Westernism that seems to be sweeping our China from its moorings; but— I must not dwell o'ermuch upon that theme, though it is a subject on which I can wax most eloquent, and I know thou desirest to hear of this house which would seem so ugly in thine eyes.

There are no quiet courtyards, no curving roofs, no softly shaded windows of shell, no rounded archways; but all is square and glaring and imposing, seeming to look coldly from its staring windows of glass at the stranger within its gates. It says loudly, "I am rich; it costs many thousands of taels to make my ugliness." For me, it is indeed a "foreign" house. Yet I will have justice within my heart and tell thee that there is much that we might copy with advantage. In place of floors of wide plain boards, and walls of wood with great wide cracks covered with embroideries and rugs, as in the Chinese homes, the floors are made of tiny boards polished until they glisten like unto the sides of the boats of the teahouse girls, and the walls are of plaster covered, as in our rooms of reception, with silk and satin, and the chairs and couches have silken tapestry to match their colour. This furniture, strange to me, is a great care, as I do not understand its usages, and it seems most stiff and formal. I hope some day to know a foreign woman on terms of friendship, and I will ask her to touch the room with her hands of knowledge, and bring each piece into more friendly companionship with its neighbour. Now chairs look coldly at tables, as if to say, "You are an intruder!" And it chills me.

This house is much more simple than our homes, because of the many modern instruments that make the work less heavy and allow it to be done by few instead of many, as is our way. It is not necessary to have a man attend solely to the lighting of the lamps. Upon the wall is placed a magic button which, touched even by the hand of ignorance, floods the room with the light of many suns. We see no more the water-carrier with his two great wooden buckets swinging from the bamboo as he comes from river or canal to pour the water into the great kangs standing by the kitchen door. Nor do we need to put the powder in it to make it clear and wholesome. That is all done by men we do not see, and they call it "sanitation." The cook needs only to turn a small brass handle, and the water comes forth as from a distant spring. It reminds me of the man who came to my father, when he was governor of Wuseh, and wished to install a most unheard-of machine to bring water to the city from the lake upon the hillside. My father listened most respectfully to the long and stupid explanation, and looked at the clear water which the foreign man produced to show what could be done, then, shaking his head, said, "Perhaps that water is more healthful, as you say, but it is to me too clear and white. It has no body, and I fear has not the strength of the water from our canals."

Another thing we do not hear is the rattle of the watchman as he makes his rounds at night, and I miss it. In far Sezchuan, on many nights when sleep was distant, I would lie and listen as he struck upon his piece of hollow bamboo telling me that all was well within our compound. Now the city has police that stand outside the gateway. Many are men from India— big black men, with fierce black beards and burning eyes. Our people hate them, and they have good cause. They are most cruel, and ill-treat all who come within their power. But we must tread with cat-like steps, as they are employed by the English, who protect them at all times. They are the private army of that nation here within our city, and at every chance their numbers are constantly increased. I do not understand this question of police. There are in thousands of our cities and villages no police, no soldiers, yet there is less lawlessness and vice in a dozen purely Chinese cities than in this great mongrel town that spends many tens of thousands of taels each year upon these guardians of the people's peace. It seems to me that this should tell the world that the force of China is not a physical force, but the force of the law-abiding instinct of a happy common people, who, although living on the verge of misery and great hunger, live upright lives and do not try to break their country's laws.

There is a garden within our walls, but not a garden of winding pathways and tiny bridges leading over lotus ponds, nor are there hillocks of rockery with here and there a tiny god or temple peeping from some hidden grotto. All is flat, with long bare stretches of green grass over which are nets, by which my children play a game called tennis. This game is foolish, in my eyes, and consists of much jumping and useless waste of strength, but the English play it, and of course the modern Chinese boy must imitate them. I have made one rule: my daughters shall not play the game. It seems to me most shameful to see a woman run madly, with great boorish strides, in front of men and boys. My daughters pout and say it is played by all the girls in school, and that it makes them strong and well; but I am firm. I have conceded many things, but this to me is vulgar and unseemly.

Need I tell thee, Mother mine, that I am a stranger in this great city, that my heart calls for the hills and the mountain-side with its ferns and blossoms? Yesterday at the hour of twilight I drove to the country in the motor (a new form of carrying chair that thou wouldst not understand— or like) and I stopped by a field of flowering mustard. The scent brought remembrance to my heart, and tears flowed from beneath my eyelids. The delicate yellow blossoms seemed to speak to me from out their golden throats, and I yearned to hold within my arms all this beauty of the earth flowering beneath my feet. We stayed until the darkness came, and up to the blue night rose from all the fields "that great soft, bubbling chorus which seems the very voice of the earth itself— the chant of the frogs." When we turned back and saw the vulgar houses, with straight red tops and piercing chimneys, I shut my eyes and in a vision saw the blue-grey houses with their curved-up, tilted roofs nestling among the groves of bamboo, and I felt that if it were my misfortune to spend many moons in this great alien city, my heart would break with longing for the beautiful home I love.

I felt sympathy with Kang Tang-li, of my father's province, who heard of a new God in Anhui. He had eaten bitter sorrow and he felt that the old Gods had forgotten him and did not hear his call, so he walked two long days' journey to find this new God who gave joy and peace to those who came to him. He arrived at eventime, the sun was setting in a lake of gold, but even with its glory it could not change the ugly square-built temple, with no curves or grace to mark it as a dwelling-place of Gods. Kang walked slowly around this temple, looked long at its staring windows and its tall and ugly spire upon the rooftree which seemed to force its way into the kindly blue sky; then, saddened, sick at heart, he turned homeward, saying deep within him no God whom he could reverence would choose for a dwelling-place a house so lacking in all beauty.

Is this a long and tiresome letter, my Honourable Mother? But thou art far away, and in thy sheltered walls yearn to know what has come to us, thy children, in this new and foreign life. It is indeed a new life for me, and I can hardly grasp its meaning. They are trying hard to force us to change our old quietude and peace for the rush and worry of the Western world, and I fear I am too old and settled for such sudden changes.

Tell Mah-li's daughter that I will send her news of the latest fashions, and tell Li-ti that the hair is dressed quite differently here. I will write her more about it and send her the new ornaments. They are not so pretty in my eyes, nor are the gowns so graceful, but I will send her patterns that she may choose.

We all give thee our greetings and touch my hand with love.
Kwei-li.

2

My Dear Mother,

I have not written thee for long, as my days have been filled with duties new and strange to me. The wives of the foreign officials have called upon me, as that appears to be their custom. It seems to me quite useless and a waste of time; but they come, and I must return the calls. I do not understand why the consuls cannot transact their business with the Governor without trying to peer into his inner life. To us a man's official life and that which lies within his women's courtyard are as separate as two pathways which never meet.

The foreign woman comes and sits upon the edge of her chair in great discomfort, vainly searching for a subject upon which we may have a common bond. I sit upon the edge of the chair from necessity, as these chairs are far too high for me, and my tiny feet hang helplessly in the air. Although the chairs are not so high or so straight and stiff as are our seats of honour, they have no footstools, and no small tables on which to lean the arm. Thou wouldst laugh at our poor feeble efforts to be agreeable one to the other. Our conversation is as foolish and as useless as would be the using of a paper lantern for the rice-mill. With all desire to be courteous and to put her at her ease, I ask about her children, the health of her honourable mother, and the state of her household. I do not ask her age, as I have learned that, contrary to our usage, it is a question not considered quite auspicious, and often causes the flush of great embarrassment to rise to the cheek of a guest. Often she answers me in "pidgin" English, a kind of baby-talk that is used when addressing servants. These foreign women have rarely seen a Chinese lady, and they are surprised that I speak English; often I have been obliged to explain that when I found that my husband's office brought him close to foreigners, and that my sons and daughters were learning the new education in which it is necessary to know other than their mother tongue, I would not be left behind within closed doors, so I too learned of English and of French enough to read and speak. I am to them a curiosity. It has not been correct in former times to know a Chinese lady socially;

and to these ladies, with their society, their calls, their dinners, and their games of cards, we within the courtyards are people from another world. They think that Chinese women are and always have been the closely prisoned slaves of their husbands, idle and ignorant and soulless, with no thoughts above their petty household cares and the strange heathen gods they worship.

Of course, these foreign women do not say these things in words, but their looks are most expressive, and I understand. I serve them tea and cake, of which they take most sparingly, and when the proper time has come they rise, trying not to look relief that their martyrdom is over. I conduct them to the doorway, or, if the woman is the wife of a great official, to the outer entrance. Then I return to my own rooms midst the things I understand; and I fear, I fear, Mother mine, that I gossip with my household upon the ways and dress and manners of these queer people from distant lands.

I have been asked to join a society of European and Chinese ladies for the purpose of becoming acquainted one with the other, but I do not think that I will do so. I believe it impossible for the woman of the West to form an alliance with the woman of the East that will be deep-rooted. The thoughts within our hearts are different, as are our points of view. We do not see the world through the same eyes. The foreign woman has children like myself, but her ambitions and her ideals for them are different. She has a home and a husband, but my training and my instincts give my home and my husband a different place in life than that which she gives to those of her household. To me the words marriage, friendship, home, have a deeper meaning than is attached to them by a people who live in hotels and public eating-places, and who are continually in the homes of others. They have no sanctity of the life within; there are no shrines set apart for the family union, and the worship of the spirits of their ancestors. I cannot well explain to thee, the something intangible, the thick grey mist that is always there to put its bar across the open door of friendship between the woman of the Occident and those of Oriental blood.

I would ask of thee a favour I wish that thou wouldst search my rooms and find the clothing that is not needed by thy women.

My house is full to overflowing. I had no idea we had so many poor relations. The poor relation of our poor relation and the cousin of our cousin's cousin have come to claim their kinship. Thy son will give no one official position nor allow them money from the public funds; but they must have clothing and rice, and I provide it. I sometimes feel, when looking into the empty rice-bin, that I sympathize with His Excellency Li Hung-chang who built a great house here, far from his home province. When asked why, unlike the Chinese custom, he builded so far from kith and kin, he answered, "You have placed the finger upon the pulse-beat the first instant. I built it far away, hoping that all the relatives of my relatives who find themselves in need, might not find the money where-with to buy a ticket in order to come and live beneath my rooftree." (With us, they do not wait for tickets; they have strong and willing feet.) I am afraid that His Excellency, although of the old China that I love, was touched with this new spirit of each member for himself that has come upon this country.

It is the good of the one instead of the whole, as in the former times, and there is much that can be said upon both sides. The family should always stand for the members of the clan in the great crises of their lives, and help to care for them in days of poverty and old age. It is not just that one should prosper while others of the same blood starve; yet it is not just that one should provide for those unwilling to help themselves. I can look back with eyes of greater knowledge to our home, and I fear that there are many eating from the bowl of charity who might be working and self-respecting if they were not members of the great family Liu, and so entitled to thy help.

It is the hour for driving with the children. We all are thine and think of thee each day.

Kwei-li.

3

My Mother,

I have such great news to tell thee that I hardly know where to begin. But, first, I will astonish thee— Ting-fang is home! Yes, I can hear thee say, "Hi yah!" And I said it many times when, the evening before last, after thy son and the men of the house-hold had finished the evening meal, and I and the women were preparing to eat our rice, we saw a darkness in the archway, and standing there was my son. Not one of us spoke a word; we were as if turned to stone; as we thought of him as in far-off America, studying at the college of Yale. But here he stood in real life, smiling at our astonishment. He slowly looked at us all, then went to his father and saluted him respectfully, came and bowed before me, then took me in his arms in a most disrespectful manner and squeezed me together so hard he nearly broke my bones. I was so frightened and so pleased that of course I could only cry and cling to this great boy of mine whom I had not seen for six long years. I held him away from me and looked long into his face. He is a man now, twenty-one years old, a big, strong man, taller than his father. I can hardly reach his shoulder. He is straight and slender, and looks an alien in his foreign dress, yet when I looked into his eyes I knew it was mine own come to me again.

No one knows how all my dreams followed this bird that left the nest. No one knows how long seemed the nights when sleep would not come to my eyes and I wondered what would come to my boy in that far-off land, a strange land with strange, unloving people, who would not care to put him on the pathway when he strayed. Thou rememberest how I battled with his father in regard to sending him to England to commence his foreign education. I said, "Is not four years of college in America enough? Why four years' separation to prepare to go to that college? He will go from me a boy and return a man. I will lose my son." But his father firmly said that the English public schools gave the ground-work for a useful life. He must form his code of honour and his character upon the rules laid down for centuries by the English, and then go to America for the education of the intellect, to learn to apply the lessons learned in England. He did not want his son to be all for present success, as is the American, or to be all for tradition, as is the Englishman, but he thought the two might find a happy meeting-place in a mind not yet well formed.

But thoughts of learning did not assuage the pain in my mother-heart. I had heard of dreadful things happening to our Chinese boys who are sent abroad to get the Western knowledge. Often they marry strange women who have no place in our life if they return to China, and who lose their birthright with the women of their race by marrying a Chinese. Neither side can be blamed, certainly not our boys. They go there alone, often with little money. They live in houses where they are offered food and lodging at the cheapest price. They are not in a position to meet women of their own class, and being boys they crave the society of girls. Perhaps the daughter of the woman who keeps the lodging-house speaks to them kindly, talks to them in the evening when they have no place to go except to a lonely, ugly room; or the girl in the shop where they buy their clothing smiles as she wraps for them their packages. Such attentions would be passed by without a thought at ordinary times, but now notice means much to a heart that is trying hard to stifle its loneliness and sorrow, struggling to learn in an unknown tongue the knowledge of the West; in lieu of mother, sister, or sweetheart of his own land, the boy is insensibly drawn into a net that tightens about him, until he takes the fatal step and brings back to his mother a woman of an alien race.

One sorrows for the girl, whatever may be her station, as she does not realize that there is no place for her in all the old land of China. She will be scorned by those of foreign birth, and she can never become one of us. Dost thou remember the wife of Wang, the secretary of the embassy at London? He was most successful and was given swift promotion until he married the English lady, whose father was a tutor at one of the great colleges. It angered Her Majesty and he was recalled and given the small post of secretary to the Taotai of our city. The poor foreign wife died alone within her Chinese home, into which no friend had entered to bid her welcome. Some say that after many moons of solitude and loneliness she drank the strong drink of her country to drown her sorrow. Perhaps it was a bridge on which she crossed to a land filled with the memories of the past which brought her solace in her time of desolation.

But I have wandered, Mother mine; my mind has taken me to England, America, to Chinese men with foreign wives, and now I will return and tell thee of thine own again, and of my son who has returned to me. When at last the Gods gave us our breath, we asked the many questions which came to us like a river that has broken all its bounds. Thy son, the father of Ting-fang, was more than angry— he was white with wrath, and demanded what Ting-fang did here when he should have been at school. My son said, and I admired the way he spoke up boldly to his father, "Father, I read each day of the progress of the Revolution, of the new China that was being formed, and I could not stay on and study books while I might be helping here." His father said, "Thy duty was to stay where I, thy father, put thee!" Ting-fang answered, "Thou couldst not have sat still and studied of ancient Greece and Rome while thy country was fighting for its life;" and then he added, most unfilially, "I notice thou art not staying in Sezchuan, but art here in Shanghai, in the centre of things. I am thy son; I do not like to sit quietly by the road and watch the world pass by; I want to help make that world, the same as thou."

His father talked long and bitterly, and the boy was saddened, and I crept silently to him and placed my hand in his. It was all I could do, for the moment, as it would not be seemly for me to take his part against his father, but— I talked to thy son, my husband, when we were alone within our chamber.

The storm has passed. His father refused to make Ting-fang a secretary, as he says the time is past when officials fill their Yamens with their relatives and friends. I think that as the days go on, he will relent, as in these troublous times a high official cannot be sure of the loyalty of the men who eat his rice, and he can rely upon his son. A Liu was never known to be disloyal.

There is too much agitation here. The officials try to ignore it as much as possible, believing that muddy water is often made clear if allowed to stand still. Yet they must be ready to act quickly, as speedily as one springs up when a serpent is creeping into the lap, because now the serpent of treachery and ingratitude is in every household. These secret plottings, like the weeds that thrust their roots deep into the rice-fields, cannot be taken out without bringing with them some grain, and many an innocent family is now suffering for the hot-headedness of its youth.

I sometimes think that I agree with the wise governor of the olden time whose motto was to empty the minds of the people and fill their stomachs, weaken their wills and strengthen their bones. When times were troublous he opened the government granaries and the crowds were satisfied.

But the people are different now; they have too much knowledge. New ambitions have been stirred; new wants created; a new spirit is abroad and, with mighty power, is over-turning and recasting the old forms and deeply rooted customs. China is moving, and, we of the old school think, too quickly. She is going at a bound from the dim light of the bean-oil brazier to the dazzling brilliance of the electric light; from the leisured slowness of the wheelbarrow pushed by the patient coolie to the speed of the modern motor-car; from the practice of the seller of herbs to the science of the modern doctor. We all feel that new China is at a great turning-point because she is just starting out on her journey that may last many centuries, and may see its final struggle tomorrow. It is of great importance that the right direction shall be taken at first. A wrong turn at the beginning, and the true pathway may never be found. So much depends upon her leaders, on men like Yuan, Wu, and thy son, my husband; the men who point out the road to those who will follow as wild fowl follow their leader. The Chinese people are keen to note disinterestedness, and if these men who have risen up show that they have the good of the people at heart much may be done. If they have the corrupt heart of many of the old-time officials, China will remain as before, so far as the great mass of her men are concerned.

I hear the children coming from their school, so I will say good-by for a time. Ting-fang sends his most respectful love, and all my household join in sending thee good wishes.

Kwei-li.

4

My Dear Mother,

Dost thou remember Liang Tai-tai, the daughter of the Princess Tseng, thine old friend of Pau-chau? Thou rememberest we used to laugh at the pride of Liang in regard to her mother's clan, and her care in speaking of her father who was only a small official in the governor's Yamen. Thou wert wont to say that she reminded thee of the mule that, when asked who was his father, answered, "The horse is my maternal uncle." She comes to see me often, and she worries me with her piety; she is quite mad upon the subject of the Gods. I often feel that I am wrong to be so lacking in sympathy with her religious longings; but I hate extremes. "Extreme straightness is as bad as crookedness, and extreme cleverness as bad as folly." She is ever asking me if I do not desire, above all things, the life of the higher road— whatever that may mean. I tell her that I do not know. I would not be rare, like jade, or common, like stone; just medium. Anyway, my days are far too full to think about any other road than the one I must tread each day in the fulfillment of the duties the Gods have given me.

Some people seem to be irreverently familiar with the Gods, and to be forever praying. If they would only be a little more human and perform the daily work that lies before them (Liang's son is the main support of the Golden Lotus Tea-house) they might let prayer alone a while without ceasing to enjoy the protection of the Gods. It is dangerous to over-load oneself with piety, as the sword that is polished to excess is sometimes polished away. And there is another side that Liang should remember, her husband not having riches in abundance: that the rays of the Gods love well the rays of Gold.

But today she came to me with her rice-bowl overflowing with her sorrows. Her son has returned from the foreign lands with the new education from which she hoped so much, but it seems he has acquired knowledge of the vices of the foreigner to add to those of the Chinese. He did not stay long enough to become Westernised, but he stayed long enough to lose touch with the people and the customs of his country. He forgets that he is not an American even with his foreign education; he is still an Oriental and he comes back to an Oriental land, a land tied down by tradition and custom, and he can not adapt himself. He tries instead, to adapt China to his half-Europeanised way of thought, and he has failed. He has become what my husband calls an agitator, a tea-house orator, and he sees nothing but wrong in his people. There is no place in life for him, and he sits at night in public places, stirring foolish boys to deeds of treason and violence. Another thing, he has learned to drink the foreign wines, and the mixture is not good. They will not blend with Chinese wine, any more than the two civilisations will come together as one.

Why did the Gods make the first draught of wine to curse the race of men, to make blind the reason, to make angels into devils and to leave a lasting curse on all who touch it? "It is a cataract that carries havoc with it in a road of mire where he who falls may never rise again." It seems to me that he who drinks the wine of both lands allows it to become a ring that leads him to the Land of Nothing, and ends as did my friend's son, with the small round ball of sleep that grows within the poppy. One morning's light, when he looked long into his own face and saw the marks that life was leaving, he saw no way except the Bridge of Death; but he was not successful.

His mother brought him to me, as he has always liked me, and is a friend (for which I sorrow) of my son. I talked to him alone within an inner chamber, and tried to show to him the error of his way. I quoted to him the words spoken to another foolish youth who tried to force the gates of Heaven: "My son, thou art enmeshed within these world's ways, and have not cared to wonder where the stream would carry thee in coming days. If thou mere human duties scorn, as a worn sandal cast aside, thou art no man but stock-stone born, lost in a selfish senseless pride. If thou couldst mount to Heaven's high plain, then thine own will might be thy guide, but here on earth thou needs must dwell. Thou canst well see that thou art not wanted in the Halls of Heaven; so turn to things yet near; turn to thy earthly home and try to do thy duty here. Thou must control thyself, there is no escape through the Eastern Gateway for the necessity of self-conquest."

He wept and gave me many promises; and I showed him that I believed in him, and saw his worth. But— we think it wiser to send him far away from his companions, who only seek to drag him down. Thy son will give to him a letter and ask the Prefect of Canton to give him work at our expense.

I felt it better that Liang Tai-tai should not be alone with her son for several hours, as her tongue is bitter and reproaches come easily to angry lips, so I took her with me to the garden of a friend outside the city. It was the Dragon Boat Festival, when all the world goes riverward to send their lighted boats upon the waters searching for the soul of the great poet who drowned himself in the olden time, and whose body the jealous Water God took to himself and it nevermore was found. Dost thou remember how we told the story to the children when the family all were with thee— oh, it seems many moons ago.

The garden of my friend was most beautiful, and we seemed within a world apart. The way was through high woods and over long green plots of grass and around queer rocks; there were flowers with stories in their hearts, and trees who held the spirits of the air close 'neath their ragged covering. Pigeons called softly to their mates, and doves cooed and sobbed as they nestled one to the other. We showed the children the filial young crow who, when his parents are old and helpless, feeds them in return for their care when he was young; and we pointed out the young dove sitting three branches lower on the tree than do his parents, so deep is his respect.

When the western sky was like a golden curtain, we went to the canal, where the children set their tiny boats afloat, each with its lighted lantern. The wind cried softly through the bamboo-trees and filled the sails of these small barks, whose lights flashed brightly from the waters as if the Spirits of the River laughed with joy.

We returned home, happy, tired, but with new heart to start the morrow's work.

Thy daughter, Kwei-li.

5

My Dear Mother,

We are in the midst of a most perplexing problem, and one that is hard for us to cope with, as it is so utterly new. My children seem to have formed an alliance amongst themselves in opposition to the wishes of their parents on all subjects touching the customs and traditions of the family. My son, as thou rememberest, was betrothed in childhood to the daughter of his father's friend, the Governor of Chili-li. He is a man now, and should fulfill that most solemn obligation that we, his parents, laid upon him— and he refuses. I can see thee sit back aghast at this lack of filial spirit; and I, too, am aghast. I cannot understand this generation; I'm afraid that I cannot understand these, my children. My boy insists that he will marry a girl of his own choice, a girl with a foreign education like unto his own. We have remonstrated, we have urged, we have commanded, and now at last a compromise has been effected. We have agreed that when she comes to us, teachers shall be brought to the house and she shall be taught the new learning. Along with the duties of wife she shall see the new life around her and from it take what is best for her to know.

I can understand his desire to have a wife with whom he may talk of the things or common interest to them both, a wife who can share with him, at least in part, the life beyond the woman's courtyard. I remember how I felt when thy son returned from foreign lands, filled with new sights, new thoughts in which I could not share. I had been sitting quietly behind closed doors, and I felt that I could not help in this new vision that had come to him. I could speak to only one side of his life, when I wished to speak to all; but I studied, I learned, and, as far as it is possible for a Chinese woman, I have made my steps agree with those or my husband, and we march close, side by side.

My son would like his wife to be placed in a school, the school from which my daughter has just now graduated; but I will not allow it. I am not in favour of such schools for our girls. It has made or Wan-li a half-trained Western woman, a woman who finds music in the piano instead of the lute, who quotes from

Shelley, and Wordsworth, instead of from the Chinese classics, who thinks embroidery work for servants, and the ordering of her household a thing beneath her great mental status.

I, of course, wish her to marry at once; as to me that is the holiest desire of woman— to marry and give men— children to the world; but it seems that the word "marry" has opened the door to floods of talk to which I can only listen in silent amazement. I never before had realised that I have had the honour of bearing children with such tongues of eloquence; and I fully understand that I belong to a past, a very ancient past— the Mings, from what I hear, are my contemporaries. And all these words are poured upon me to try to persuade me to allow Wan-li to become a doctor. Canst thou imagine it? A daughter of the house of Liu a doctor! From whence has she received these unseemly ideas except in this foreign school that teaches the equality of the sexes to such an extent that our daughters want to compete with men in their professions! I am not so much of the past as my daughter seems to think; for I believe, within certain bounds, in the social freedom of our women; but why commercial freedom? For centuries untold, men have been able to support their wives; why enter the market-places? Is it not enough that they take care of the home, that they train the children and fulfill the duties of the life in which the Gods place women? My daughter is not ugly, she is most beautiful; yet she says she will not marry. I tell her that when once her eyes are opened to the loved one, they will be closed to all the world beside, and this desire to enter the great world of turmoil and strife will flee like dew-drops before the summer's dawn. I also quoted her what I told Chih-peh many moons ago, when he refused to marry the wife thou hadst chosen for him: "Man attains not by himself, nor woman by herself, but like the one-winged birds of the ancient legend, they must rise together."

My daughter tossed her head and answered me that those were doubtless words of great wisdom, but they were written by a man long dead, and it did not affect her ideas upon the subject of her marriage.

We dare not insist, for we find, to our horror, that she has joined a band of girls who have made a vow, writing it with their blood, that, rather than become wives to husbands not of their own choice, they will cross the River of Death. Fifteen girls, all friends of my daughter, and all of whom have been studying the new education for women, have joined this sisterhood; and we, their mothers, are in despair. What can we do? Shall we insist that they return to the old regime and learn nothing but embroidery? Why can they not take what is best for an Eastern woman from the learning of the West, as the bee selects honey from each flower, and leave the rest? It takes centuries of training to change the habits and thoughts of a nation. It cannot be done at once; our girls have not the foundation on which to build. Our womanhood has been trained by centuries of caressing care to look as lovely as nature allows, to learn obedience to father as a child, to husband as a wife, and to children when age comes with his frosty fingers.

Yet we all know that the last is a theory only to be read in books. Where is there one so autocratic in her own home as a Chinese mother? She lives within its four walls, but there she is supreme. Her sons obey her even when their hair is touched with silver. Did not thy son have to ask thy leave before he would decide that he could go with His Highness to the foreign lands? Did he not say frankly that he must consult his mother, and was he not honoured and given permission to come to his home to have thy blessing? Dost thou remember when Yuan was appointed secretary to the embassy in London, and declined the honour because his mother was old and did not wish her only son to journey o'er the seas; he gave up willingly and cheerfully the one great opportunity of his life rather than bring sorrow to the one who bore him.

A similar case came to our ears but a few days since. Some priests of a foreign mission came to my husband and wished him to intercede, as Governor, and command the Taotai of Soochow to sell to them a piece of land on which to erect a temple of their faith. When the Taotai was asked why he was so persistent in his refusal to carry out the promise of the man before him in the office, he told the Governor that the temple where his mother worshipped was in a direct line with the proposed new foreign house of worship. His mother feared that a spire would be placed upon its rooftree that would intercept the good spirits of the air from bringing directly to her family rooftree the blessings from the temple. My husband tried to persuade him that the superstitions of a woman long in years should not stand in the way of a possible quarrel with men of a foreign power, but the Taotai only shrugged his shoulders and said, "What can I do? She is my mother. I cannot go against her expressed commands;" and— the temple to the foreign God will not be built.

But it is as foolish to talk to Wan-li as "to ask the loan of a comb from a Buddhist nun." She will not listen; or, if she does, a smile lies in the open lily of her face, and she bows her head in mock submission; then instantly lifts it again with new arguments learned from foreign books, and arguments that I in my ignorance cannot refute.

I feel that I am alone on a strange sea with this, my household; and I am in deadly fear that she will do some shocking thing, like those girls from the school in Foochow who, dressed in their brothers' clothing, came to Nanking and asked to be allowed to fight on the side of the Republic. Patriotism is a virtue, but the battle-field is man's place. Let the women stay at home and make the bandages to bind the wounded, and keep the braziers lighted to warm returning men.

I will not write thee more of troubles, but I will tell thee that thy box of clothing came and is most welcome; also the cooking oil, which gave our food the taste of former days. The oils and sauces bought at shops are not so pure as those thy servants make within the compound, nor does the cook here prepare things to my taste. Canst send me Feng-yi, who understands our customs? Thy son has no great appetite, and I hope that food prepared in homely ways may tempt him to linger longer at the table. He is greatly over-worked, and if he eat not well, with enjoyment of his rice, the summer will quite likely find him ill.

Thy daughter and thy family who touch thy hand, Kwei-li

6

My Dear Mother,

Thy letter came, and I thank thee for thy advice. It is most difficult to act upon. I cannot shut Wan-li within an inner chamber, nor can I keep her without rice until she sees the wisdom of her ways. The times are truly different; we mothers of the present have lost our power to control our children, and cannot as in former days compel obedience. I can only talk to her; she laughs. I quote to her the words of the Sage: "Is any blessing better than to give a man a son, man's prime desire by which he and his name shall live beyond himself; a foot for him to stand on, a hand to stop his falling, so that in his son's youth he will be young again, and in his strength be strong." Be the mother of men; and I hear that, that is China's trouble. She has too many children, too many thousands of clutching baby fingers, too many tiny mouths asking for their daily food. I am told, by this learned daughter of mine, that China has given no new thing to the world for many tens of centuries. She has no time to write, no time to think of new inventions; she must work for the morrow's rice. "How have you eaten?" Is the salutation that one Chinese makes to another when meeting on a pathway; and in that question is the root of our greatest need. I am told that we are a nation of rank materialists; that we pray only for benefits that we may feel or see, instead of asking for the blessings of the Spirit to be sent us from above; that the women of my time and kind are the ruin of the country, with our cry of sons, sons!

But if our girls flaunt motherhood, if this thought of each one for himself prevails, what will become of us, a nation that depends upon its worship of the ancestors for its only practical religion? The loosening of the family bonds, the greater liberty of the single person, means the lessening of the restraining power of this old religion which depends upon the family life and the unity of that life. To do away with it is to do away with the greatest influence for good in China today. What will become of the filial piety that has been the backbone of our country? This family life has always been, from time immemorial, the foundation-stone of our Empire, and filial piety is the foundation-stone of the family life.

I read not long since, in the Christian's Sacred Book, the commandment, "Honour thy father and thy mother, that thy days may be long in the land which the Lord thy God hath given thee," and I thought that perhaps in the observance of that rule is to be found one of the chief causes for the long continuance of the Chinese Empire. What is there to compare in binding power to the family customs of our people? Their piety, their love one for the other and that to which it leads, the faithfulness of husband to his wife—all these, in spite of what may be said against them by the newer generation, do exist and must influence the nation for its good. And this one great fact must be counted amongst the forces, if it is not the greatest force, which bind the Chinese people in bonds strong as ropes of twisted bamboo.

Our boys and girls will not listen; they are trying to be what they are not, trying to wear clothes not made for them, trying to be like nations and people utterly foreign to them; and they will not succeed. But, "into a sack holding a ri, only a ri will go," and these sacks of our young people are full to overflowing with this, which seems to me dearly acquired knowledge, and there is not room for more. Time will help, and they will learn caution and discretion in life's halls of experience, and we can only guard their footsteps as best we may.

In the meantime, Mother mine, my days are full and worried, and I, as in the olden time, can only come to thee with my rice-bowl filled with troubles and pour them all into thy kindly lap. It is my only comfort, as thy son is bitter and will not talk with patience, and it would not be seemly for me to open wide my heart to strangers; but I know thou lovest me and art full of years and knowledge and will help me find the way.

Kwei-li.

7

My Dear Mother,

These are most troublous times, and thy son is harassed to the verge of sickness. Shanghai is filled with Chinese who come seeking foreign protection. Within the narrow confines of the foreign settlements, it is said, there are nearly a million Chinese, half of them refugees from their home provinces, fearing for their money or their lives, or both. The great red houses on the fashionable streets, built by the English for their homes, are sold at fabulous prices to these gentlemen, who have brought their families and their silver to the only place they know where the foreign hand is strong enough to protect them from their own people. There are many queer tales; some are simply the breath of the unkind winds that seem to blow from nowhere but gain in volume with each thing they touch. Tan Toatai, who paid 300,000 taels for his position as Toatai of Shanghai, and who left for his home province with 3,000,000 taels, as the gossips say, was asked to contribute of his plenty for the help of the new government. He promised; then changed his mind, and carefully gathered all his treasures together and left secretly one night for Shanghai. Now he is in fear for his life and dares not leave the compound walls of the foreigner who has befriended him.

It makes one wonder what is the use of these fortunes that bring endless sorrow by the misery of winning them, guarding them, and the fear of losing them. They who work for them are as the water buffalo who turns the water-wheel and gets but his daily food and the straw-thatched hut in which he rests. For the sake of this food and lodging which falls to the lot of all, man wastes his true happiness which is so hard to win.

These Chinese of the foreign settlements seem alien to me. Yuan called upon thy son the other day, and had the temerity to ask for me— a most unheard-of thing. I watched him as he went away, dressed in European clothes, as nearly all of our younger men are clothed these days, and one would never know that he had worn his hair otherwise than short. There are no more neatly plaited braids hanging down the back, and the beautiful silks and satins, furs and peacock feathers are things of the past. These peacock feathers, emblems of our old officialdom, are now bought by foreign ladies as a trimming on their hats. Shades of Li Hungchang and Chang Chih-tung! What will they say if looking over the barriers they see the insignia of their rank and office gracing the glowing head-gear of the tourists who form great parties and come racing from over the seas to look at us as at queer animals from another world?

It is not only the men who are copying the foreign customs and clothing. Our women are now seen in public, driving with their husbands, or walking arm in arm upon the public street. I even saw a Chinese woman driving that "devil machine," a motor-car, with her own hands. She did not seem a woman, but an unsexed thing that had as little of woman-hood as the car that took her along so swiftly. I promised to send Tah-li the new hair ornaments, but there are no hair ornaments worn now. The old jewels are laid aside, the jade and pearls are things of the past. The hair is puffed and knotted in a way most unbecoming to the face. It is neither of the East nor of the West, but a half-caste thing, that brands its wearer as a woman of no race.

Dost thou remember the story over which the Chinese in all the Empire laughed within their sleeves? Her Majesty, the Empress Dowager, was on most friendly terms with the wife of the Minister of the United States of America, and on one occasion gave her as a gift a set of combs enclosed within a box of silver. The foreign lady was delighted, and did not see the delicate sarcasm hidden within the present. Combs— the foreign ladies need them! We Chinese like the locks most smoothly brushed and made to glisten and shine with the scented elm, but they, the foreign ladies, allow them to straggle in rude disorder around their long, grave faces, which are so ugly in our eyes.

Thou hast asked me for the latest style in dress. It is impossible to say what is the latest style. Some women wear a jacket far too short and trousers tight as any coat sleeve. The modest ones still cover them with skirts; but I have seen women walking along the street who should certainly stay within the inner courtyard and hide their shame. For those who wear the skirt, the old, wide-pleated model has gone by, and a long black skirt that is nearly European is now worn. It is not graceful, but it is far better than the trousers worn by women who walk along so stiffly upon their "golden lilies." These tiny feet to me are beautiful, when covered with gay embroidery they peep from scarlet skirts; but they too are passing, and we hear no more the crying of the children in the courtyards. I am told that the small-footed woman of China is of the past, along with the long finger-nails of our gentlemen and scholars; and I am asked why I do not unbind my feet. I say, "I am too old; I have suffered in the binding, why suffer in the unbinding?" I have conceded to the new order by allowing unbound feet to all my girls, and everywhere my family is held up as an example of the new Chinese. They do not know of the many bitter tears I have shed over the thought that my daughters would look like women of the servant class and perhaps not make a good marriage; but I was forced to yield to their father, whose foreign travel had taught him to see beauty in ugly, natural feet. Even now, when I see Wan-li striding across the grass, I blush for her and wish she could walk more gracefully. My feet caused me many moons of pain, but they are one of the great marks of my lady-hood, and I yet feel proud as I come into a room with the gentle swaying motions of the bamboo in a breeze; although my daughter who supports me takes one great step to five of mine.

The curse of foot binding does not fall so heavily upon women like myself, who may sit and broider the whole day through, or, if needs must travel, can be borne upon the shoulders of their chair bearers, but it is a bane to the poor girl whose parents hope to have one in the family who may marry above their station, and hoping thus, bind her feet. If this marriage fails and she is forced to work within her household, or, even worse, if she is forced to toil within the fields or add her mite gained by most heavy labour to help fill the many eager mouths at home, then she should have our pity. We have all seen the small-footed woman pulling heavy boats along the tow-path, or leaning on their hoes to rest their tired feet while working in the fields of cotton. To her each day is a day of pain; and this new law forbidding the binding of the feet of chil-dren will come as Heaven's blessing. But it will not cease at once, as so many loudly now proclaim. It will take at least three generations; her children's children will all quite likely have natural feet. The people far in the country, far from the noise of change and progress, will not feel immediately that they can wander so far afield from the old ideas of what is beautiful in their womanhood.

I notice, as I open wide my casement, that the rain has come, and across the distant fields it is falling upon the new-sown rice and seems to charm the earth into the thought that spring is here, bringing forth the faint green buds on magnolia, ash, and willow. Dost thou remember the verse we used to sing:

"Oh she is good, the little rain, and well she knows our need, Who cometh in the time of spring to aid the sun-drawn seed. She wanders with a friendly wind through silent heights unseen, The furrows feel her happy tears, and lo, the land is green!"

I must send a servant with the rain coverings for the children, that they may not get wet in returning from their schools.

We greet thee, all.

Kwei-li.

8

My Dear Mother,

Last night I heard a great wailing in the servants' courtyard, and found there the maid of thy old friend, Tang Tai-tai. She came from Nanking to us, as she has no one left in all the world. She is a Manchu and has lived all her life in the Manchu family of Tang within the Tartar city of Nanking. It seems the soldiers, besieging the city, placed their guns on Purple Hill, so that they would cause destruction only to the Tartar city, and it was levelled to the ground. No stone remains upon another; and the family she had served so faithfully were either killed in the battle that raged so fiercely, or were afterward taken to the grounds of Justice to pay with their life for the fact that they belonged to the Imperial Clan. She is old, this faithful servant, and now claims my protection. It is another mouth to feed; but there is so much unhappiness that if it were within my power I would quench with rains of food and drink the anguish this cruel war has brought upon so many innocent ones. A mat on which to sleep, a few more bowls of rice, these are the only seeds that I may sow within the field of love, and I dare not them withhold.

I am most sorrowful for these poor Manchus. For generations they have received a pension from the government; to every man-child an allowance has been made; and now they find themselves with nothing. Even their poor homes are piles of stone and rubbish. What will they do to gain their food in this great country which is already full to over-flowing? They are so pitiful, these old men and women thrown so suddenly upon the world. Their stories pierce my marrow, and I would that my sleeve were long and wide enough to cover all the earth and shelter these poor helpless ones. One old man— his years must have been near eighty— came to our door for help. I talked to him and found that, until his sons were killed before his eyes, his home torn to the ground, he had never been without the city's walls. He said, just like a child, "Why should I go? My wife, my sons, my home, my all, were within the walls; why go outside?"

Each hour brings us fresh rumours of the actions of the rebels,

Poor Liang Tai-tai was here and in the sorest trouble. Her husband and her brother were officers in the army of Yuan, and when in Ranking were shot along with twenty of their brother officers, because they would not join the Southern forces. To add to China's trouble, the Southern pirates are attacking boats; and I am glad to say, although it sounds most cruel, that the government is taking measures both quick and just. Ten men were captured and were being brought by an English ship to Canton, and when in neutral waters it is said a Chinese gunboat steamed alongside with an order for the prisoners. As they stepped upon the Chinese boat, each man was shot. The English were most horrified, and have spoken loudly in all the papers of the acts of barbarism; but they do not understand our people. They must be frightened; especially at a time like this, when men are watching for the chance to take advantage of their country's turmoil.

These pirates of Canton have always been a menace. Each village in that country must be forever on the defensive, for no man is safe who has an ounce of gold. When father was the prefect of Canton, I remember seeing a band of pirates brought into the Yamen, a ring of iron around the collarbone, from which a chain led to the prisoner on either side. It was brutal, but it allowed no chance of escape for these men, dead to all humanity, and desperate, knowing there awaited them long days of prison, and in the end they knew not what.

In those days imprisonment was the greatest of all evils; it was not made a place of comfort. For forty-eight long hours, the man within the clutches of the law went hungry; then, if no relative or friend came forth to feed him, he was allowed one bowl of rice and water for each day. A prison then meant ruin to a man with money, because the keepers of the outer gate, the keepers of the inner gate, the guardian of the prison doors, the runners in the corridor, the jailer at the cell, each had a hand that ached for silver. A bowl of rice bought at the tea-shop for ten cash, by the time the waiting hungry man received it, cost many silver dollars. Yet a prison should not be made a tempting place of refuge and vacation; if so in times of cold and hunger it will be filled with those who would rather suffer shame than work.

Another thing the people who cry loudly against our old-time Courts of Justice do not understand, is the crushing, grinding, naked poverty that causes the people in this over-crowded province to commit most brutal deeds. The penalties must match the deeds, and frighten other evil-doers. If the people do not fear death, what good is there in using death as a deterrent; and our Southern people despise death, because of their excessive labour in seeking the means of life. But— what a subject for a letter! I can see thee send for a cup of thy fragrant sun-dried tea, mixed with the yellow flower of the jessamine, to take away the thoughts of death and evil and the wickedness of the world outside thy walls. It will never touch thee, Mother mine, because the Gods are holding thee all safe within their loving hands.

Thy daughter, Kwei-li.

9

My Mother,

I have most joyful news to tell thee. My father has arrived! He came quite without warning, saying he must know the changing times from word of mouth instead of reading it in papers. He has upset my household with his many servants. My father keeps to his old ways and customs and travels with an army of his people. His pipe man, his hat man, his cook, his boy— well, thou rememberest when he descended upon us in Sezchuan— yet he could bring ten times the number, and his welcome would be as warm. The whole town knows he is our guest, and foreigners and Chinese have vied one with the other to do him honour. The foreign papers speak of him as "the greatest Chinese since Li Hung-chang," and many words are written about his fifty years' service as a high official. The story is retold of his loyalty to Her Majesty at the time of the Boxer uprising, when he threatened the foreigners that if Her Majesty was even frightened, he would turn his troops upon Shanghai and drive the foreigners into the sea. I wonder if the present government can gain the love the Dowager Empress drew from all who served her.

My father was the pioneer of the present education, so say the papers, and it is remembered that his school for girls in the province where he ruled, nearly caused him the loss of his position, as His Excellency, Chang Chih-tung, memorialised the throne and said that women should not have book learning; that books would only give them a place in which to hide their threads and needles. It is also said of him that he was always against the coming of the foreigners. They could obtain no mine, no railway, no concession in a province where he was representing his Empress. China was closed, so far as lay within his power, to even men of religion from other lands. It was he who first said, "The missionary, the merchant, and then the gunboat."

My father will not talk with men about the present trials of China; he says, most justly, that he who is out of office should not meddle in the government. When asked if he will give the results of his long life and great experience to the Republic, he answers that he owes his love and loyalty to the old regime under which he gained his wealth and honours; and then he shakes his head and says he is an old man, nothing but wet ashes. But they do not see the laughter in his eyes; for my father "is like the pine-tree, ever green, the symbol of unflinching purpose and vigorous old age."

So many old-time friends have been to see him. Father, now that the heavy load of officialdom is laid aside, delights to sit within the courtyards with these friends and play at verse-making. No man of his time is found lacking in that one great attribute of a Chinese gentleman. He has treasures of poetry that are from the hands of friends long since passed within the Vale of Longevity. These poems are from the pens of men who wrote of the longing for the spiritual life, or the beauties of the world without their doors, or the pleasure of association with old and trusted friends. I read some scrolls the other day, and it was as though "aeolian harps had caught some strayed wind from an unknown world and brought its messages to me." It is only by the men of other days that poetry is appreciated, who take the time to look around them, to whom the quiet life, the life of thought and meditation is as vital as the air they breathe. To love the beautiful in life one must have time to sit apart from the worry and the rush of the present day. He must have time to look deep within his hidden self and weigh the things that count for happiness; and he must use most justly all his hours of leisure, a thing which modern life has taught us to hold lightly.

But with our race verse-making has always been a second nature. In the very beginning of our history, the Chinese people sang their songs of kings and princes, of the joys of family life and love and home and children. It is quite true that they did not delve deep into the mines of hidden passions, as their songs are what songs should be, telling joyful tales of happiness and quiet loves. They are not like the songs of warrior nations, songs of battle, lust and blood, but songs of peace and quiet and deep contentment. When our women sang, like all women who try to voice the thoughts within them, they sang their poems in a sadder key, all filled with care, and cried of love's call to its mate, of resignation and sometimes of despair.

My father learned to love the poets in younger days, but he still reads them o'er and o'er. He says they take him back to other years when life with all its dreams of beauty, love, and romance, lay before him. It brings remembrance of youth's golden days when thoughts of fame and mad ambition came to him with each morning's light. This father of mine, who was stiffly bound with ceremony and acts of statecraft for ten long months of the year, had the temerity to ask two months' leave of absence from his duties, when he went to his country place in the hills, to his "Garden of the Pleasure of Peace." It was always in the early spring when "that Goddess had spread upon the budding willow her lovely mesh of silken threads, and the rushes were renewing for the year." He sat beneath the bamboos swaying in the wind like dancing girls, and saw the jessamine and magnolia put forth their buds.

What happy days they were when father came! For me, who lived within the garden all the year, it was just a plain, great garden; but when he came it was transformed. It became a place of rare enchantment, with fairy palaces and lakes of jewelled water, and the lotus flowers took on a loveliness for which there is no name. We would sit hand in hand in our gaily painted tea-house, and watch the growing of the lotus from the first unfurling of the leaf to the fall of the dying flower. When it rained, we would see the leaves raise their eager, dark-green cups until filled, then bend down gracefully to empty their fulness, and rise to catch the drops again.

The sound of the wind in the cane-fields came to us at night-time as we watched the shimmer of the fireflies. We sat so silently that the only thing to tell us that the wild duck sought his mate amidst the grass, was the swaying of the reed stems, or the rising of the teal with whirring wings.

My father loved the silence, and taught me that it is in silence, in the quiet places, rather than on the house-tops, that one can hear the spirit's call, and forget the clanging of the world. It is the great gift which the God of nature alone can give, and "he has found happiness who has won through the stillness of the spirit the Perfect Vision, and this stillness comes through contentment that is regardless of the world."

He often said to me that we are a caravan of beings, wandering through life's pathways, hungering to taste of happiness, which comes to us when we find plain food sweet, rough garments fine, and contentment in the home. It comes when we are happy in a simple way, allowing our wounds received in life's battles to be healed by the moon-beams, which send an ointment more precious than the oil of sandalwood.

I could go on for pages, Mother mine, of the lessons of my father, this grand old man, "who steeled his soul and tamed his thoughts and got his body in control by sitting in the silence and being one with nature, God, the maker of us all." And when I think of all these things, it is hard to believe that men who love the leisure, the poetry, the beautiful things of life, men like my father, must pass away. It seems to me it will be a day of great peril for China, for our young ones, when these men of the past lose their hold on the growing mind. As rapidly as this takes place, the reverence for the old-time gentleman, the quiet lady of the inner courtyards, will wane, and reverence will be supplanted by discourtesy, faith by doubt, and love of the Gods by unbelief and impiety.

Yet they say he does not stand for progress. What is progress? What is life? The poet truly cries: "How short a time it is that we are here! Why then not set our hearts at rest, why wear the soul with anxious thoughts? If we want not wealth, if we want not power, let us stroll the bright hours as they pass, in gardens midst the flowers, mounting the hills to sing our songs, or weaving verses by the lily ponds. Thus may we work out our allotted span, content with life, our spirits free from care."

My father has a scroll within his room that says:

"For fifty years I plodded through the vale of lust and strife, Then through my dreams there flashed a ray of the old sweet peaceful life. No scarlet tasselled hat of state can vie with soft repose; Grand mansions do not taste the joys that the poor man's cabin knows. I hate the threatening clash of arms when fierce retainers throng, I loathe the drunkard's revels and the sound of fife and song; But I love to seek a quiet nook, and some old volume bring, Where I can see the wild flowers bloom and hear the birds in spring."

Ah, dear one, my heart flows through my pen, which is the messenger of the distant soul to thee, my Mother.

Kwei-li.

10

My Dear Mother,

My days are passed like a water-wheel awhirl, and I can scarcely find time to attend to the ordinary duties of my household. I fear I seem neglectful of thee, and I will try to be more regular with my letters, so that thou wilt not need reproach me. Tonight my house is quiet and all are sleeping, and I can chat with thee without the many interruptions that come from children, servants, and friends during the waking hours.

I have had callers all the day; my last, the wife of the Japanese Consul, who brought with her two children. They were like little butterflies, dressed in their gay kimonas and bright red obis, their straight black hair framing their tiny elfin faces. I was delighted and could scarcely let them go. Their mother says she will send to me their photographs, and I will send them to thee, as they seem children from another world. They are much prettier, in my eyes, than the foreign children, with their white hair and colourless, blue eyes, who always seem to be clothed in white. That seems not natural for a child, as it is our mourning colour, and children should wear gay colours, as they are symbols of joy and gladness.

My husband watched them go away with looks of hatred and disdain within his eyes, and when I called them Butterflies of Gay Nippon, he gave an ejaculation of great disgust, as at this time he is not o'erfond of the Japanese. He believes, along with others, that they are helping the rebels with their money, and we know that many Japanese officers are fighting on the side of the Southern forces. He could not forget the words I used, "Dainty Butterflies," and he said that these dainty butterflies are coming far too fast, at the rate of many tens of thousands each year, and they must be fed and clothed and lodged, and Japan is far too small. These pretty babies searching for a future home are China's greatest menace. Japan reels that her destiny lies here in the Far East, where she is overlord, and will continue as such until the time, if it ever comes, when new China, with her far greater wealth and her myriads of people, dispute the power of the little Island. At present there is no limit to Japan's ambition. Poor China! It will take years and tens of years to mould her people into a nation; and Japan comes to her each year, buying her rice, her cotton and her silk.

These wily merchants travel up her path-ways and traverse her rivers and canals, selling, buying, and spreading broadcast their influence. There are eight thousand men of Japan in Shanghai, keen young men, all looking for the advantage of their country. There is no town of any size where you cannot find a Japanese. They have driven the traders of other nationalities from many places; the Americans especially have been compelled to leave; and now there is a bitter struggle between the people from the British Isles and the Japanese for the trade of our country. In the olden time the people from Great Britain controlled the trade of our Yang-tse Valley, but now it is almost wholly Japanese.

The British merchant, in this great battle has the disadvantage of being honest, while the trader from Japan has small thoughts of honesty to hold him to a business transaction. We say here, "One can hold a Japanese to a bargain as easily as one can hold a slippery catfish on a gourd." The Sons of Nippon have another point in their favour: the British merchant is a Westerner, while the Japanese uses to the full his advantage of being an Oriental like ourselves. Trade— trade— is what Japan craves, and it is according to its need that she makes friends or enemies. It is her reason for all she does; her diplomacy, her suavity is based upon it; her army and her vast navy are to help gain and hold it; it is the end and aim of her ambitions.

We, Chinese, have people— millions, tens of millions of them. When they are better educated, when China is more prosperous, when new demands and higher standards of living are created, when the coolie will not be satisfied with his bowl of rice a day and his one blue garment, then possibilities of commerce will be unlimited. Japan sees this with eyes that look far into the future, and she wants to control this coming trade— and I fear she will. She has an ambition that is as great as her overpowering belief in herself, an ambition to be in the East what England is in the West; and she is working patiently, quietly, to that end. We fear her; but we are helpless. I hear the men talk bitterly; but what can they do. We must not be another Corea; we must wait until we are strong, and look to other hands to help us in our struggle.

We hope much from America, that country which has so wonderful an influence upon us, which appeals to our imagination because it is great and strong and prosperous. The suave and humorous American, with his easy ways, is most popular with our people, although he cannot always be trusted nor is his word a bond. He is different from the man of England, who is not fond of people not of his own colour and will not try to disguise the fact. He is cold and shows no sympathy to those of an alien race, although we must admit he always acts with a certain amount of justice. America is contemptuous of China and her people, but it is a kindly contempt, not tinged with the bitterness of the other Powers, and we hope, because of that kindliness and also because of trade interests (the American is noted for finding and holding the place that yields him dollars), she will play the part of a kindly friend and save China from her enemies who are now watching each other with such jealous eyes. There is another reason why we like America: she does not seem to covet our land. There is no Shang-tung nor Wei-hai-wei for her. I would that she and England might form a bond of brotherhood for our protection; because all the world knows that where Germany, Russia, or Japan has power, all people from other lands are barred by close-shut doors.

Since hearing my husband talk I see those babies with other eyes, with eyes of knowledge and dislike. I see them becoming one of the two great classes in Japan— merchants with grasping hands to hold fast all they touch, or men of war. There is no other class. And, too, they have no religion to restrict them, irreverence already marks their attitude toward their gods. They will imitate and steal what they want from other countries, even as their ancestors took their religion, their art, their code of ethics, even their writing, from other peoples. Their past is a copy of the East; their present is an attempt to be a copy of the West. They cannot originate or make a thing from within them-selves.

Their lives are coarse and sordid when stripped of the elaborate courtesy and sham politeness that marks their dealings with the outside world. Their courtesy, what is it? This thin veneer of politeness is like their polished lacquer that covers the crumbling wood within. But we have a proverb, "Even a monkey falls"; and some distant day the Western world that thinks so highly of Japan will see beneath the surface and will leave her, and the great pagoda she has builded without foundation will come tumbling down like the houses of sand which my children build in the garden. It will be seen that they are like their beautiful kimonas, that hang so gracefully in silken folds. But take away the kimonas, and the sons and daughters of that Empire are revealed in all their ugliness— coarse, heavy, sensual, with no grace or spirit life to distinguish them from animals.

Do I speak strongly, my Mother? We feel most strongly the action of the Japanese in this, our time of trouble. We have lost friends; the husbands, brothers, fathers of our women-folk are lying in long trenches because of training given to our rebels by members of that race. I should not speak so frankly, but it is only to thee that I can say what is within my heart. I must put the bar of silence across my lips with all save thee; and sitting here within the courtyard I hear all that goes on in Yamen, shop, and women's quarters. One need not leave one's doorway to learn of the great world. I hear my sons speak of new China, and many things I do not understand; my husband and his friends talk more sedately, for they are watching thoughtful men, trying hard to steer this, our ship of State, among the rocks that now beset it close on every side. My daughters bring their friends, my servants their companions, and the gossip of our busy world is emptied at my feet.

The clock strikes one, and all the world's asleep except, Kwei-li.

11

Dear Mother,

She is here, my daughter-in-law, and I can realise in a small degree thy feelings when I first came to thy household. I know thou wert prepared to give me the same love and care that my heart longs to give to this, the wife of my eldest son. I also know how she feels in this strange place, with no loved faces near her, with the thought that perhaps the new home will mean the closed doors of a prison, and the husband she never saw until the marriage day the jealous guardian thereof. I have tried to give her welcome and let her see that she is heart of our hearts, a part of us.

She is different from the young girls I have seen these latter days, different from my daughters, and— I may say it to thee, my Mother— a sweeter, dearer maiden in many ways. She has been trained within the courtyards in the old-fashioned customs that make for simplicity of heart, grace of manner, that give obedience and respect to older people; and she has the delicate high-bred ways that our girls seem to feel unnecessary in the hurry of these days. She takes me back to years gone by, where everything is like a dream, and I can feel again the chair beneath me that carried me up the mountain-side with its shadowing of high woods, and hear the song of water falling gently from far-off mountain brooks, and the plaintive cry of flutes unseen, that came to welcome me to my new home.

With her dainty gowns, her tiny shoes, her smooth black hair, she is a breath from another world, and my sons and daughters regard her as if she were a stray butterfly, blown hither by some wind too strong for her slight wings. She is as graceful as the slender willow, her youthful charm is like the cherry-tree in bloom, and the sweet thoughts natural to youth and the springtime of life, flow from her heart as pure as the snow-white blossoms of the plum-tree. She does not belong to this, our modern world; she should be bending with iris grace above goldfish in the ponds, or straying in gardens where there are lakes of shimmering water murmuring beneath great lotus flowers that would speak to her of love.

We are all more than charmed, and gather to the sunshine she has brought. As they knelt before us for our blessing, I thought what a happy thing is youth and love. "Kings in their palaces grow old, but youth dwells forever at contentment's side."

But I must tell thee of the marriage. Instead of the red chair of marriage, my new daughter-in-law was brought from the house of her uncle in that most modern thing, a motor-car. I insisted that it should be covered with red satin, the colour of rejoicing; and great rosettes trailed from the corners to the ground. The feasting was elaborate and caused me much care in its preparation, as not only had been provided the many different kinds of food for our Chinese friends, but foreigners, who came also, were served with dishes made expressly for them, and with foreign wines, of which they took most liberally. The Europeans, men and women, ate and drank together with a freedom that to me is most unseemly, and I cannot understand the men who have no pride in their women's modesty but allow them to sit at table with strange men close by their side. Behind the archway, we Chinese women "of the old school," as my daughter calls us, feasted and laughed our fill, just as happy as if parading our new gowns before the eyes of stranger-men.

Li-ti is delighted with thy gift, the chain of pearls. It is a most appropriate present, for "pearls belong of right to her whose soul reflects the colour of youth's purity"; and I, I am so happy in this new life that has come to dwell beneath our rooftree. I had many fears that she would not be to my liking, that she would be a modern Chinese woman; and another one, oh, Mother mine, would fill to overflowing my bowl of small vexations; but the place is perfumed by her scent, the scent of sandalwood, which represents the China that I love, and flowers of jessamine and purple hyacinths and lilies-of-the-valley, which speak to us of youth and spring and love and hope.

Thy daughter, who gives the messages from all thy family, who touch thy hand with deep respect.

12

My Dear Mother,

I am sorry that thou hast been troubled by news of the fighting within the province. All is well with us, as we sent thee word by telegraph. If anything happens that touches any of thy household, we will send thee word at once.

This town is a hotbed of rebellion, and it is all because the rebels have been enabled to perfect their plans through the existence of the foreign settlements. How I dislike these foreigner adventurers! I wish they would take their gilded dust, their yellow gold, and leave us to our peace; but they walk our streets as lords and masters, and allow the plotting traitors to make their plans, and we are helpless. If I were China's ruler and for one day had power, there would not be one white man left within the borders of my country. We hear each day of friends who give their lives on the field of battle, these battles and this conflict which would not be present with us were it not for the foreign powers, who within these settlements, protect the low-browed ruffians who are plotting China's ruin.

Did I say I disliked these foreigners? How mild a word! Thou, in Sezchuan, far from the touch of the alien life, hast never seen these people who cause us so much trouble. How can I describe them to thee so that thou wilt understand? They are like unto the dragons of the earth, for ugliness. Men have enormous stature and mighty strength, and stride with fierce and lordly steps. Their faces have great noses between deep-set eyes, and protruding brows, and ponderous jaws like animals— symbols of brute force which needs but to be seen to frighten children in the dark. We are the gentler race, and we feel instinctively the dominating power of these men from over the seas, who all, American, Russian, German, English, seem to be cast in the same brutal mould. Their women have long, horse-like faces, showing the marks of passion and discontent, which they try to cover with the contents of the powder-jar and with rouge; they are utterly unlike the women of our race, who are taught to express no hate, no love, nor anything save perfect repose and gentleness, as befits true ladyhood.

One has but to see a Chinese gentleman, with his easy manners, composed, self-contained, with a natural dignity, to know that we are better trained than the people from the West. It is because we are true idealists. We show it in our grading of society. With us the scholar is honoured and put first, the farmer second, the artisan third, and the merchant and the soldier last. With them, these worshippers of the dollar, the merchant is put first, and the man to guard that dollar is made his equal! That is a standard for a nation! The barterer and the murderer; let others follow where they lead.

These foreigners rate China low, who have never met a Chinese gentleman, never read a line of Chinese literature, and who look at you in ignorance if you mention the names of our sages. They see no Chinese except their servants, and they judge the world about them from that low point of view. I know a lady here who is a leader in their society, a woman who has lived within our land for many tens of years; when asked to meet a prince of our house Imperial, she declined, saying she never associated with Chinese. A prince to her was no more than any other yellow man; she said she would as soon think of meeting her gate coolie at a social tea. How can there be a common meeting-ground between our people and the average European, of whom this woman is a representative and who is not alone in her estimation of the people amongst whom she lives but whom she never sees. They get their knowledge of China from servants, from missionaries who work among the lower classes, and from newspaper reports that are always to the disadvantage of our people.

More and more the West must see that the East and West may meet but never can they mingle. Foreigners can never enter our inner chamber; the door is never wholly opened, the curtain never drawn aside between Chinese and European. The foreign man is a materialist, a mere worshipper of things seen. With us "the taste of the tea is not so important as the aroma." When Chinese gentlemen meet for pleasure, they talk of poetry and the wisdom of the sages, of rare jade and porcelains and brass. They show each other treasures, they handle with loving fingers the contents of their cherished boxes, and search for stores of beauty that are brought to light only for those who understand. But when with foreigners, the talk must be of tea, its prices, the weight of cotton piece goods, the local gossip of the town in which they live. Their private lives are passed within a world apart, and there is between these men from different lands a greater bar than that of language— the bar of mutual misunderstanding and lack of sympathy with the other race.

Poor China! She is first clubbed on the head and then stroked on the back by these foreigners, her dear friends. Friends! It is only when the cold season comes that we know the pine-tree and the cypress to be evergreens, and friends are known in adversity. The foreigners who profess to be our friends are waiting and hoping for adversity to come upon us, that they may profit by it. They want our untouched wealth, our mines of coal and iron and gold, and it is upon them they have cast their eyes of greed.

The foreigners have brought dishonesty in business dealings to our merchants. At first, the trader from the foreign land found that he could rely on old-time customs and the word of the merchant to bind a bargain; but what did the Chinese find? There are no old-time customs to bind a foreigner, except those of bond and written document. He has no traditions of honour, he can be held by nothing except a court of law. For years the word "China" has meant to the adventurers of other lands a place for exploitation, a place where silver was to be obtained by the man with fluent tongue and winning ways. Even foreign officials did not scruple to use their influence to enter trade.

An old case has recently come before the Governor. It has been brought many times to the ears of the officials, but they have said nothing, for fear of offending the Great Government whose representative is involved in the not too pleasant transaction. One of our great inland cities had no water nearer than the river, several miles away. A foreign official with a machine of foreign invention digged deep into the earth and found pure, clear water. Then he thought, "If there is ater here for me, why not for all this great city of many tens of thousands?" Which was a worthy thought, and he saw for himself great gains in bringing to the doors of rich and poor alike the water from the wells. He told the Taotai that he would go to his country and bring back machines that would make the water come forth as from living springs. The official met his friends and the plan was discussed and many thousands of taels were provided and given into the hands of the official from over the seas. The friends of the Taotai felt no fear for their money, as the official signed a contract to produce water from the earth, and he signed, not as a simple citizen but as the representative of his government, with the great seal of that government attached to the paper. Of course our simple people thought that the great nation was behind the project; and they were amazed and startled when, after a trip to his home land and a return with only one machine, a few holes were made but no water found, and the official announced that he was sorry but there was nothing more that he could do. He did not offer to return the money, and in his position he could not be haled into a court of law; there was nothing for his dupes to do but to gaze sadly into the great holes that had taken so much money, and remember that wisdom comes with experience.

"When a man has been burned once with hot soup he forever after blows upon cold rice"; so these same men of China will think o'erlong before trusting again a foreigner with their silver.

Thy son has been trying to settle another case. Some men from America went to Ningpo, and talked long and loud of the darkness of the city, its streets dangerous in the night-time, its continual fires caused by the flickering lamps of oil that are being so constantly overturned by the many children. They told the officials that the times were changing, that to walk the streets with a lighted lantern in the hand is to lose step with the march of progress. They showed the benefits of the large lights of electricity blazing like a sun on each corner of the great city, making it impossible for robbers and evil-doers to carry on their work in darkness. They promised to turn night-time into day, to put white lights in Yamen, office, and house-hold. There should be a light beneath each rooftree, at no greater expense than the bean-oil lamp. They were most plausible, and many thousands of silver dollars were brought forth and given to the men as contract money. They left us to buy machinery; the years have passed; they never have returned. Ningpo still has streets of darkness, men still walk abroad with lighted lanterns, the bean-oil lamp is seen within the cottage and— will be until the hills shall fade, so far as the officials are concerned, who once dreamed dreams of a city lit by the light as of myriad suns.

How can the missionaries have the face to come here with their religion, when the dissolute white man is in every port manifesting a lust and greed and brutality which Chinese are accustomed to associate with the citizenship and religion attributed to Christianity. No wonder it is hard for them to make converts among the people who have business dealings with these men from Christian nations.

But China will not forever bear the ill-treatment of men from Western lands. She is awake to all the insults; she has learned in the bitter halls of experience. She sleeps no longer; she will rise in self-defense and fight aggression; and the nations who have misused her must remember that when she moves it will be the movement of a mighty people aroused by the thought of their great wrongs. She is peaceful and long-suffering, but she is different from the old-time China. She has now a national spirit that has been brought about by better means of communication between provinces. In the olden time it was difficult for one part or the Empire to know the conditions in another. But now the telegraph and the daily newspaper come to all the smallest villages. I am sure that the watchman by thy outer gate reads as he guards thy household, and learns in far Sezchuan what has happened today in Peking, or the Southern city of Canton, and the news is discussed in the tea-shops and on corners by men from farm and shop and office.

The foreigners are mistaken in their belief that China can never be united. She has been one for centuries, in beliefs, in morals, in education, and in religion, and now she will be more united in her stand against the hated white man who covets her treasures. She may quarrel with her brothers within her borders; but that is nothing but a family feud, and in time of danger from outside, like all families, she will unite to fight for her own until the last red lantern fades and the morning star is shining. Enough of politics and bitterness! I hear thy son, who is coming for his evening cup of tea.

Thy daughter, Kwei-li.

13

My Dear Mother,

The times here are very bad; people are fleeing from the inland cities and coming to Shanghai by the thousands. The place is crowded to suffocation.

Wu Ting-fang was here and talked long into the night with my husband. My son, who, I am afraid, does not think too highly of this great man, says that he is with the party that is "on top," that he spends most of his time sitting on the fence— whatever that may mean. I drove past his house the other day and did not see him sitting on the fence, but on his veranda, calmly drinking tea.

Sun Yat-sen has violated his word of honour and has joined the Southern forces. We feel he has acted most dishonourably and (my son again) should have "staid bought." Gossips say he received many millions of taels, presumably for the railroads, but that was only an excuse to slip the money into his wide and hungry pockets.

It is decided to send my son to Canton, into the office of the governor of that province. We are glad to get him away from Shanghai, which is a nest of adders and vipers, conspiring and raising their poisonous heads in the dark. One does not know whom to trust, or who may prove to be a traitor.

Li-ti, his wife, wishes to go with him, and weeps the whole day through because we will not permit it. She is not well, and we tell her she will not be really separated from her husband, because, as the poets tell us, people who love, though at a distance from each other, are like two lutes tuned in harmony and placed in adjoining rooms. When you strike the kung note on one, the kung note on the other will answer, and when you strike the cho note on the one the cho note on the other will give the same sound. They are both tuned to the same pitch, when the influence of the key-note, love, is present.

I took my son apart the other night and said, "I am thy mother and I want to speak words to thee straight from the heart. Thou art to have the joy of work, and remember the pride of work lies in the thought, 'For me alone is the task.'" I tried to make him understand that praise, glory, and honours are good, but they do not make for long life, and especially in these times it is better to work quietly without attracting too much attention. It is more safe, for "he who raises himself on tiptoe cannot stand, and he who stretches his legs wide apart cannot walk."

His father was especially anxious that he be not pierced with the arrow of treachery that poisons the blood and finds the weak spot in the armour of so many of our young men. He told him to keep himself above suspicion, to avoid those entangled in the nets of double dealing of whom one is uncertain, because "the red glow of the morning sun seems to stain even the pure whiteness of the new-fallen snow."

Why, Mother-mine, didst thou send the old priest from the temple down here? He abides in the courtyard, squatting on his heels, serving the spirits neither of Heaven nor of earth, but he sits and talks and talks and talks with the women of the courtyards. There are some of them I would fain send to a far-off province, especially Fang Tai, the mother of our gateman.

"A woman with a long tongue is a flight of steps leading to calamity."

This priest of thine has been quarrelling with her now over the question of the son of Wong Tai, who is accused of being on too friendly terms with some of the leaders of the rebellion. He made the unfortunate remark that perhaps the man was innocent but "one does not arrange his head-dress under an apricot-tree, nor his foot-gear in a melon patch, if he wishes to be above suspicion," and this simple remark has called down upon his priestly head the wrath of all the women. I think he will go to the monastery within the city to pass the night— at least if he has wisdom equal to his years.

Yesterday I thought that I might make some use of him, and I felt when he was working he would not be stirring up the courtyards. I bade him write the Sage's words upon a scroll of satin for my boy to take with him to his new home. He did it very beautifully, as he is a real artist with the brush. This is the reading of the scroll:

"There are three things for a man to guard against: The lusts of the flesh in early years, The spirit of combativeness in middle-age, And ambition as the years go on. There are three things to command your reverence: The ordinances of Heaven, Great men, and the words of the sages. There are three times three things to be remembered: To be clear in vision, Quick in hearing, Kindly in expression, Respectful in demeanour, True in word, Serious in duty, Inquiring in doubt, Self-controlled in anger, And just and fair when the chair of success is before your door."

I made a roll of it and placed it upon his desk, and when he opened it he found within another scroll of silk, the same in colour, size, and finish, written by his most unfilial sisters, which read:

"Remember that thou art young. What thou dost know is not to be compared, With what thou dost not know."

It made him angry at first, but I do not know but that the shorter scroll contains the greater wisdom.

I am anxious for this boy of mine, who is starting to sail his ship of manhood across the Broad River of Life in these most perilous times. I think he is strong enough to conquer all, but I have lighted candles and bought fine incense to persuade the Gods to temper winds to untried hands.

Thy daughter, Kwei-li.

14

My Dear Mother,

I have not written thee for several days. We are in Nanking, where my husband is presiding at a meeting of the officials in order to discuss the question of a compromise, or to try in some way to settle the questions that are causing this dreadful rebellion, without more loss of life. He is also acting as judge in the case of some of the men who have been caught pillaging and destroying the homes of the innocent people. It is hard for him to act with strict justice, remembering the many friends he has lost, and it is necessary to see things without their individuality in order to be wise in all judgments. I came, ostensibly to see the friends of my childhood, but really to take care of thy son and see that he eats with regularity and takes his rest. He is working far too hard. He gives himself to whatever task arrives, greedy for the work, like one who lusts in the delight of seeing tasks accomplished. But he is trusted by all, both sides agreeing to rest on his decisions, all realising that personal feeling is put far into the background of his mind when the interests of new China are at stake.

We are in the Yamen where I lived as a young girl, but now all is changed. Instead of the old guard of honour, with their great flapping hats, their gaily decorated jackets, baggy trousers tucked into velvet boots, pennants flying from their spear-points as their small ponies dashed madly in front of the official carriage, we were met by a body of foreign-dressed soldiers who conducted us with military precision quite different from the old-time dash and lack of discipline.

Inside the Yamen, also, things are different. Everything is orderly and moves with a machine-like regularity that seems totally foreign to an Eastern official's residence. There is not the democracy of other days; the man from the street, the merchant or the coolie with his burden on his shoulders, did not follow us into the courtyards to see what was being done, nor were there crowds of idle men gazing with mild curiosity at the visitors to their city.

We hear much of the old-time power of the officials; but

things are not nearly so democratic under this new government as in former times, when, it is true, the governor had power of life and death, but still was obliged to deal leniently with his people. A little larger demand for tribute, a case of rank injustice, and he became the object of the people's wrath and would quite likely see his Yamen in a blaze, or pay with his life for his greed. The masses held real power within their hands. If their officials did not deal justly with them, they caused a riot, and if the frightened official could not still it within a certain time, he was told that he evidently could not control his people and so was removed.

My husband inspected the regiments stationed here. I saw them from a veranda in the Yamen where we women were unseen. Fifteen thousand men marched past him; and they were a sight for one who loves his country. They were all young men, no one seeming to be over twenty-five, and as they marched my heart was filled with pride and hope in them. I thought, it is of just such men, such sons of peasants and working people, that Japan made her army that gained a victory over one of the greatest nations in the Western world. Why cannot we, with our unlimited numbers, make an army that will cause our country to be respected and take its place among the powers of the world? We have the men, myriads and myriads of them; men who are used to hardship and privation in their daily life, who, on a bowl of rice, a morsel of dried fish, can fight the whole day through. Our men are not accustomed to the luxuries of the foreigners, who, even in times of war, carry great stores of what seems to Eastern nations, unnecessary baggage. With them their endless string of wagons is their greatest pitfall, and with us these latter could be reduced to the smallest count.

Yet we hear on every hand that the courage of the Chinese soldier is held at low value. But why? When sent unarmed, or with guns for which there were no bullets, into the Japanese war, against troops with the latest inventions in weapons to kill, the only thing to be done was to retreat. But when they are paid, fed, and armed, and have leaders who will go to the front with them, instead of saying, "There is the enemy. Charge! I will go back to the hills and await your hour of glory," they are found to be courageous to the verge of fanaticism. Under trusted leaders there is no forlorn hope or desperate service for which they would not volunteer. Let them have confidence in their new generals, and, even though not understanding the cause, they will make the best soldiers in the world.

But I must not talk to thee of war; we want not more bloodshed and the fatherless homes and lean years that follow in the track of great armies. Yet, if we cannot be without it, let it serve war's ends— the ultimate safety of our people, and bring them peace and tranquillity, their heart's desire.

I visited the ruined homes of friends of mine, who are no more. It made me feel that life is nothing but a mirage, a phantom, or as foam, and "even as all earthly vessels made on the potter's wheel must end by being broken, so end the lives of men." I went out to the home of Yuan Tai-tai, who, to my childish mind was the great lady of my dreams. I can close my eyes and see her still, like a brilliant butter-fly, dressed in her gay brocades, her hair twined with jewels of pearl and jade; with hand in mine she wandered o'er her garden, bending over goldfish ponds, or clipping fading flowers from off their stems. There reigned a heavy silence in her palace, with its memories, that seemed full of sadness and a vague regret, reminding me of an old blue China bowl which a hand of other days had filled with roses. The flowers trying to struggle from beneath the thorns and brambles that always come where troops are quartered, seemed to say, "Behold, they are not here who once have cared for us and cherished us, but the gardens breathe of them and we are fragrant for their sakes." I picked a branch of cherry-blossoms, and swiftly fell the perfumed petals to the ground— symbols of the dainty lives that bloomed so short a time in this fair garden of my lady. Liu Che, the poet of the olden time, seems to have been speaking of this, my friend, when he says:

"The sound of rustling silk is stilled, With dust the marble courtyard filled; No footfalls echo on the floor, Fallen leaves in heaps block up the door... For she, my pride, my lovely one is lost."

We went from Yuan's palace to the Temple of Kwan-yin, which I often visited as a child. It also was a ruin, but it spoke to me of the dead thousands of weary feet that had climbed the steps leading to its shrines; of the buried mothers who touched the floor before its altars with reverent heads and asked blessings on their children's lives; of their children, taught to murmur prayers to the Mother of all Mercies, who held close within her loving heart the sorrows, hopes, and fears of woman's world. Ghosts of these spirits seemed to follow as we wandered through deserted court-yards, and an odour as of old incense perfumed the air. I went out and stood upon the tortoise that is left to guard the ruined temple; the great stone tortoise that is the symbol of longevity of our country, that even armies in their wrath cannot destroy.

From the gateway we could see the river, a gleaming thread of silver, and the hillsides, tree clad, flower wreathed, painted with the colours that the Gods give to the spring— the spring that "thrills the warm blood into wine." But I miss the natural songs that should float upward from the valley, and down the reed-strewn banks of the canals, where labourers in olden days were happy in their toil.

Even as we left the place the pattering rain-drops came as rice grains falling upon the threshing-floor, and the hills seemed "folding veils of sorrow round their brows." It was brought to our remembrance that we must return to a city where war and famine may come thundering at her gates, and we must stand with help-less hands.

Dear Mother mine, stay upon thy flower-scented balustrade, and drink great draughts of that wine of spring, the vintage of the wise, that the Gods give to thee freely in thy mountain home, and leave to younger hands the battles with the world. Thou must not come; write no more that thou wouldst be amongst us. We love thee dearly, but we would cherish thee and keep thee from all care.

Kwei-li.

15

My Dear Mother,

I have had a most interesting day, and I hasten to tell thee all about it. I have just returned from opening a home for motherless children, given by a mission of a foreign land. It is a beautiful thought, and a kindly one, to give a home to these poor waifs of an alien land, all in the name of their Saviour of the World. I saw for the first time a picture of this Christ, with little children around Him. The message I read within His eyes seemed to be: "I will be father and mother, father and mother and playmate to all little children." The words of the Japanese poet describe Him: "He was caressing them kindly, folding His shining robes round them; lifting the smallest and frailest into His bosom, and holding His staff for the tumblers to clutch. To His long gown clung the infants, smiling in response to His smile, glad in His beauteous compassion."

I looked at the picture and at the people around me on the platform, and wondered why in all the Christian world that claims this loving Master there should be such exceeding bitterness between His followers. How can they expect us to believe in this great Teacher when they themselves are doubtful of his message, and criticise quite openly their Holy Book? If it is true, should education and science make its teaching less authentic? We do not want a religion that is uncertain to its own people, yet we take with many thanks what it can give us, the things we understand, such as their schools and hospitals. Where there is pain or ignorance, there is no distinction in the God that brings relief. We may not believe in the doctrines that we are taught in the waiting-rooms of their hospitals, but we do believe in the healing power of the medicines that are brought by religious zeal from over the seas.

If their teaching has not as yet made many converts, the effect has been great in the spread of higher ideals of education, and much of the credit for the progress of our modern life must be given to the mission schools, which, directly or indirectly, have opened new pathways in the field of education for our country, and caused the youth of China to demand a higher learning throughout the land. This aggressive religion from the West, coupled with the education that seems to go hand in hand with it, is bound to raise the religious plane of China by forcing our dying faiths to reassume higher and higher forms in order to survive.

But I believe that these teachers from the foreign lands should understand better the religions they are so anxious to displace, and instead of always looking for the point of difference or weakness in our faith, should search more anxiously for the common ground, the spark of the true light that may still be blown to flame, finding the altar that may be dedicated afresh to the true God.

Every religion, however imperfect, has something that ought to be held sacred, for there is in all religions a secret yearning after the unknown God. This thought of God "is an elixir made to destroy death in the world, an unfailing treasure to relieve the poverty of mankind, a balm to allay his sickness, a tree under which may rest all creatures wearied with wanderings over life's pathways. It is a bridge for passing over hard ways, open to all wayfarers, a moon of thought arising to cool the fever of the world's sin, and whatever name His followers may call Him, he is the one True God of all mankind."

Whether we see the coolie bowing his head before the image of the Lord of Light, the Buddha, or the peasant woman with her paper money alight in the brazier at the feet of Kwan-yin, we ought to feel that the place where he who worships stands, is holy ground. We hear it said that he is worshipping an image, an idol, a thing of stone or wood or clay. It is not so; he is thinking far beyond the statue, he is seeing God. He looks upwards towards the sky and asks what supports that cup of blue. He hears the winds and asks them whence they come and where they go. He rises for his toil at break of day and sees the morning sun start on his golden journey. And Him who is the cause of all these wonders, he calls his Life, his Breath, his Lord of All. He does not believe that the idol is his God. "'Tis to the light which Thy splendour lends to the idol's face, that the worshipper bends."

The difference between us all lies not in the real teaching of our Holy Men, Confucius, Buddha, Lao Tze, or Christ, but in the narrowness of the structure which their followers have built upon their words. Those sages reared a broad foundation on which might have been built, stone by stone, a mighty pagoda reaching to the skies. There could have been separate rooms, but no closed doors, and from out the pointed roofs might have pealed the deep-toned bells caught by every wandering breeze to tell the world that here spoke the Truth or the One Great God. But, instead, what have they done? The followers have each built separately over that portion which was the work of their own Master. The stories have grown narrower and narrower with the years; each bell rings out with its own peculiar tone, and there is no accord or harmony.

I do not dispute with those who have found a healing for themselves. To us our religion is something quite inseparable from ourselves, something that cannot be compared with anything else, or replaced ith anything else. It is like our bodies. In its form it may be like other bodies, but in its relation to ourselves it stands alone and admits of no rival; yet the remedy that has cured us should not be forced upon a people, irrespective of their place, their environment or their temperament.

We of the East "have sounded depth on depth only to find still deeper depths unfathomed and profound," and we have learned to say that no sect or religion can claim to be in possession of all the Truth. Let the teachers from other countries learn of our doctrines. Let them learn of Buddha. To one who reads his pure teaching, nothing so beautiful, nothing so high, has been heard in all the world. We admit that, little by little, changes have come, simplicity has been lost, and with every addition something departed from its purity and it became stained. Yet I believe that much of the kindliness, much of the gentleness now so marked in Chinese nature, may be traced to the teaching of this great apostle of peace and quietude.

That other great religion, the religion of the Way, has become steeped in superstition and has been made a reproach in all our land. Yet Lao Tze had noble sentiments and lofty thoughts that have helped generations of mankind in many struggles.

Confucius, it is said, presented high ideals without the breath of spirit; his system was for the head and did not feed the heart; yet he taught that, from the highest in the land to the lowest worker in the field, personal virtue, cleanness of heart and hands, is to be held the thing of greatest value. Men are urged to cherish all that is of good in them, to avoid evil living, to cultivate right feeling, and to be true and faithful to their tasks.

We should not value the teaching of our religion "as a miser values his pearls and jade, thinking their value lessened if pearls and jade are found in other parts of the world." But the searcher after Truth will welcome any true doctrine, and believe it no less precious because it was spoken by Buddha, Lao Tze, Confucius or Christ. We should not peer too closely to learn what the temple may enshrine, but "feel the influence of things Divine and pray, because by winding paths we all may reach the same great Ocean's shore." We all are searchers for the Way. Whence do I come; where do I go? In this passage from the unknown to the unknown, this pilgrimage of life, which is the straight path, which the true road— if indeed there be a Way? Such are the questions that all the world is asking. What is the true answer; where may we find it? Whose holy book holds the key that will open wide the door?

All have a hunger of the soul for something beside life's meat and drink; all want a remedy for the sorrows of the world. The Buddhists believe that it can be found in the destruction of desire, by renouncing the world and following the noble path of peace until death shall open the portals of the unknowable, everlasting stillness from which there is no return. The Confucianists say the remedy is found within the world by fulfilling all its duties and leaving to a greater Justice the future and its rewards. The Christians give a whispered message of hope to the lonely soul beating against the bars of the world about him, and say that a life of love and joy and peace is the gift of their great Messenger, and when the years have passed that He stands within an archway to welcome those, His chosen, to a land of bliss where we shall meet all who have loved us and whom we have loved in life, and gaze upon His face.

Which is the Way, which path to God is broad enough for all the world?

Kwei-li.

16

My Dear Mother,

I received thy letter which was full of reproaches most unjust. I have not broken my word, given to thee so long ago. I opened the home for friendless children, not because it belonged to a mission of a foreign religion, but because I think it a most worthy cause. There are many homeless little ones in this great city, and these people give them food and clothing and loving care, and because it is given in the name of a God not found within our temples, is that a reason for withholding our encouragement?

Thou hast made my heart most heavy. Twenty-five years ago, when my first-born son was taken from me, I turned from Gods who gave no comfort in my time of need: all alone with hungry winds of bitterness gnawing the lute strings of my desolate mother-heart, I stood upon my terrace, and fought despair. My days were without hope and my nights were long hours filled with sorrow, when sleep went trailing softly by and left me to the old dull pain of memory. I called in anguish upon Kwan-yin, and she did not hear my prayer. The painted smile upon her lips but mocked me, and in despair I said, "There are no Gods," and in my lonely court of silent dreams I lost the thread of worldly care until my tiny bark of life was nearly drifting out upon the unknown sea.

Thou rememberest that the servants brought to me from out the market-place the book of the foreign God, and in its pages I woke to life again. I looked once more from out my curtained window, and saw the rosy glow of dawn instead of grey, wan twilights of the hopeless days before me; and, as on a bridge half seen in shadows dim, I returned to the living world about me. Thou saidst nothing until it had brought its healing, then thou tookest the book and kept it from me. Thou toldst me with tears that it would bring thine head in sorrow to thy resting-place upon the hillside if I left the Gods of my ancestors and took unto my heart the words and teachings of the God of an alien race. I promised thee that I would not cause thee grief, and I have kept my word.

In my ignorance I have longed for knowledge, for some one to explain the teaching that rolled away for me the rush of troubled waters that flooded all my soul; but as I looked about me and saw the many warring factions that follow the great Teacher of love and peace, I did not know which way to turn, which had the truth to give me; and I wanted all, not part. I have this book, and have not sought for wisdom from outside, but only search its pages to find its messages to me.

Thou must not say I have deserted China's Gods, nor is it just to write that my children are wandering from the Way. I have observed the feasts and fastings; each morn the Household God has rice and tea before him; the Kitchen God has gone with celebrations at springtime to the spirit up above. The candles have been lighted and the smoke of incense has ascended to propitiate the God of Light, Lord Buddha, and Kwan-yin, and my children have been taught their prayers and holy precepts. It is not my fault, nor shouldst thou blame it to my teaching if rites and symbols have lost their meaning, and if the Gods of China are no longer strong enough to hold our young.

Oh, Mother mine, thou knowest I would not cause thee sorrow, and thou hast hurt me sorely with thy letter of bitterness and reproach. If thou couldst have seen within my heart these many ears, and known the longing for this light that came to me in darkness, then thou wouldst not have burned the book that brought me hope and life again when all seemed gone.

Thou askest me to promise thee anew that I will not trouble thy last few years with thoughts that seem to thee a sacrilege and a desecration of thy Gods. Thou art the mother of my husband, and 'tis to thee I owe all loyalty and obedience. I promise thee, but— that which is deep within my heart— is mine.

Thy daughter, Kwei-li.

17

My Dear Mother,

I, thy son's wife, have been guilty of the sin of anger, one of the seven deadly sins— and great indeed has been my anger. Ting-fang has been bringing home with him lately the son of Wong Kai-kia, a young man who has been educated abroad, I think in Germany. I have never liked him, have looked upon his aping of the foreign manners, his half-long hair which looks as if he had started again a queue and then stopped, his stream of words without beginning and without end, as a foolish boy's small vanities that would pass as the years and wisdom came. But now— how can I tell thee— he asks to have my daughter as his wife, my Luh-meh, my flower. If he had asked for Man-li, who wishes to become a doctor, I might have restrained my anger; but, no, he wants the beauty of our house-hold, and for full a space of ten breaths' breathing-time, I withheld my indignation, for I was speechless. Then I fear I talked, and only stopped for lack of words. My son is most indignant, and says I have insulted his dear friend. His dear friend indeed! He is so veiled in self-conceit that he can be insulted by no one; and as for being a friend, he does not know the word unless he sees in it something to further his own particular interests.

I told my son that he is a man who leads a life of idleness and worse. The tea-house knows him better than his rooftree. He is most learned and has passed safely many examinations, and writes letters at the end of his name, and has made an especial study of the philosophers of the present time; and because of this vast amount of book learning and his supposedly great intelligence he is entitled to indulgence, says my son, and should not be judged by the standards that rule ordinary people, who live upon a lower plane. I say that his knowledge and greater intelligence (which latter I very much doubt) increase his responsibilities and should make of him an example for the better living of men.

A clever bad man is like vile characters scrawled in ink of gold, and should be thrown aside as fit only for the braziers.

He is handsome in my daughter's eyes; but I say virtue is

within the man, not upon his skin. He fascinates my younger sons with his philosophy and his tea-house oratory. I do not like philosophy, it is all marked with the stamp of infidelity and irreligion. It is rarely that a man devotes himself to it with-out robbing himself of his faith, and casting off the restraints of his religion; or, if they do not lose it utterly, they so adulterate it with their philosophy that it is impossible to separate the false from the true. The reading of philosophic writings, so full of vain and delusive reasonings, should be forbidden to our young folk, just as the slippery banks of a river are forbidden to one who knows not how to swim. I will have none of them in our library, nor will I allow their father to read them where his sons can see him. The snake-charmer should not touch the serpents before his child's eyes, knowing that the child will try to imitate him in all things.

It is "as pouring water in a frog's face" to talk to these, my children, who think a man, with words upon his lips, a sage. I say a dog is not a good dog because he is a good barker, nor should a man be considered a good man because he is a good talker; but I see only pity in their faces that their mother is so far behind the times. These boys of ours are so much attracted by the glimpses they have had of European civilisation, that they look down upon their own nationality. They have been abroad only long enough to take on the veneer of Western education; it is a half-and-half knowledge; and it is these young men who become the discontented ones of China. When they return they do not find employment immediately, since they have grown out of touch with their country and their country's customs. They feel that they should begin at the top of the ladder, instead of working up slowly, rung by rung, as their fathers did before them. They must be masters all at once, not realising that, even with their tiny grains of foreign knowledge, they have not yet experience to make them leaders of great enterprises or of men; yet they know too much to think of going back into their father's shop.

I realise that the students who go abroad from China have many difficulties to overcome. It is hard to receive their information and instruction in a language not their mother tongue. They have small chance to finish their education by practical work in bank or shop or factory. They get a mass of book knowledge and little opportunity to practise the theories which they learn, and they do not understand that the text-book knowledge is nearly all foreign to their country and to the temperament of their race. I often ask, when looking at my son, what is his gain? I presume it is in securing a newer, broader point of view, an ability to adjust himself to modern conditions, and a wider sympathy with the movements of the world.

China has for centuries been lost to the world by reason of her great exclusion, her self-satisfaction and blind reliance upon the ways marked out for her by sages of other days. These young men, with the West in their eyes, are coming back to shock their fathers' land into new channels. The process may not be pleasant for us of the old school, but quite likely it is necessary. Yet, I feel deep within me, as I look at them, that these new Westernised East-erners with their foreign ways and clever English are not to be the final saviours of China. They are but the clarion voices that are helping to awake the slumbering power. China must depend upon the firmer qualities of the common people, touched with the breath of the West.

It is with great sorrow that we mothers and fathers see our boys and girls, especially those who return from abroad, neglecting and scoffing at our modes of education that have endured and done such noble work for centuries past. I know it is necessary to study things modern to keep up with the demands of the times; but they can do this and still reserve some hours for the reading of the classics. Instead of always quoting Byron, Burns, or Shelley, as do my son and daughter, let them repeat the beautiful words of Tu Fu, Li Po, Po Chu-i, our poets of the golden age.

In no country is real learning held in higher esteem than in China. It is the greatest characteristic of the nation that, in every grade of society, education is considered above all else. Why, then, should our young people be ashamed of their country's learning? The Chinese have devoted themselves to the cultivation of litera-ture for a longer period by some thousands of years than any existing nation. The people who lived at the time of our ancestors, the peoples of Egypt, the Greeks, the Romans, have disappeared ages ago and have left only their histories writ in book or stone. The Chinese alone have continued to give to the world their treasures of thought these five thousand years. To literature and to it alone they look for the rule to guide them in their conduct. To them all writing is most sacred. The very pens and papers used in the making of their books have become objects of veneration. Even our smallest village is provided with a scrap-box into which every bit of paper containing words or printed matter is carefully placed, to await a suitable occasion when it may be reverently burned.

Change is now the order of the day, educationally as well as politically. We do not hear the children shouting their tasks at the top of their voices, nor do they learn by heart the thirteen classics, sitting on their hard benches within the simple rooms with earthen floor, where the faint light comes straggling through the unglazed windows on the boy who hopes to gain the prize that will lead him to the great Halls of Examination at Peking. If, while there, he is favoured by the God of Learning and passes the examination, he will come back to his village an honour to his province, and all his world will come and do him reverence, from the viceroy in his official chair to the meanest worker in the fields. These old-time examinations are gone, the degrees which were our pride have been abolished, the subjects of study in the schools have been completely changed. The privileges which were once given our scholars, the social and political offices which were once open to the winner of the highest prize, have been thrown upon the altar of modernity. They say it is a most wise move and leads to the greater individualism, which is now the battle-cry of China. The fault of the old examination, we are told, is the lack of original ideas which might be expressed by a student. He must give the usual interpretations of the classics. Now the introduction of free thought and private opinion has produced in China an upheaval in men's minds. The new scholars may say what they think wisest, and they even try to show that Confucius was at heart a staunch republican, and that Mencius only thinly veiled his sentiments of modern philosophy.

Perhaps the memory work of the Chinese education was

wrong; but it served its purpose once, if tales are true.

It is said that many hundreds of years ago, the founder of the Chinese dynasty, the man of pride who styled himself Emperor the First, conceived the idea of destroying all literature which was before his reign, so that he might be regarded by posterity as the founder of the Chinese Empire. It is believed by many Chinese scholars that this wicked thing was done, and that not a single perfect copy of any book escaped destruction. He even went so far as to bury alive above five hundred of the best scholars of the land, that none might remain to write of his cruel deed. But the classics had been too well learned by the scholars, and were reproduced from memory to help form the minds of China for many tens of years. This could be done today if a similar tragedy were enacted. Thousands of boys have committed the great books to heart, and this storing in the mind of enormous books has developed in our race a marvellous memory, if, as others say, it has taken away their power of thinking for themselves.

Which is the best? Only time will tell. But we are told that the literati of China, the aristocracy of our land, must go. Yet, as of old, it is the educated men who will move China. Without them, nothing can be done, for the masses will respect education and the myriads will blindly follow a leader whom they feel to be a true scholar; and it will be hard to change the habits of a people who have been taught for centuries that education is another word for officialdom.

This new education, in my mind, must not be made so general; it must be made more personal. Three things should be taken into account: who the boy is, where he is, and where he is going. It is not meet to educate the son of my gate-keeper the same as my son. He should be made a good workman, the best of his kind, better to fill the place to which the Gods have called him. Give our boys the modern education, if we must, but remember and respect the life work each may have to follow. Another thing we should remember: the progress in the boy's worldly knowledge should not make him hard in his revolt against his Gods, nor should his intelligence be freed without teaching him self-control. That is fatal for our Eastern race. Let him learn, in his books and in his laboratories, that he moulds his destiny by his acts in later life, and thus gain true education, the education of the soul as well as of the mind.

I have written thee a sermon, but it is a subject on which we mothers are thinking much. It is before us daily, brought to our courtyards by our sons and daughters, and we see the good and the evil of trying to reach at a single bound the place at which other nations have at last arrived after centuries of weary climbing.

I must go to the women's quarters and stop their chattering. Oh, Mother mine, why didst thou send to me that priest of thine?

Kwei-li.

18

Dear Mother,

I must introduce thee to thy new daughter-in-law. Yes, I can see thee start. I will tell thee quickly. Thy son hath not taken to himself another wife, but it is I, Kwei-li, who should be made known to thee anew. Kwei-li, the wife of the Governor of Kiangsi, who has become so foreignised that the mother of her husband would never know her. If things keep on the path they have gone for these last few moons, I fully expect thou wilt see me with that band of women who are making such a great outcry for their rights and freedom. I cannot even explain them to thee, as thou wouldst not understand.

My last adventure in the ways or the modern woman is in relation to the courtship of my son. Tang-si, my second son, is in love; and I, his mother, am aiding and abetting him, and allowing him to see his sweet-heart in the foreign way. I know thou wilt blush when thou readest this; but I have been in the hands of the Gods and allowed not to speak of "custom," or propriety, and when I have tried to reason with my son and talk to him in regard to what is seemly, he laughs at me and calls me pet names, and rubs my hair the wrong way and says I am his little mother. I knew that astounding fact long years ago, and still I say that is no reason why I should go against all customs and traditions of my race.

I told him I was taught that men and women should not sit together in the same room, nor keep their wearing apparel in the same place, nor even cleanse them in the same utensils. They should not look upon each other, or hand a thing directly from man to woman hand. I was taught that it was seemly and showed a maidenly reserve to observe a certain distance in my relations even with my husband or my brothers, but I have found that the influence of reason upon love is like that of a raindrop upon the ocean, "one little mark upon the water's face and then it disappears."

Now I will tell thee all about it. Tang-si came to me one day, and after speaking of many things of no importance, he finally said, "Mother, wilt thou ask Kah-li, Wu Tai-tai's daughter, here to tea?" I said, "Why, is she a friend of thy sister's?" He said, while looking down upon the floor, "I do not know, but— but— she is a special friend of mine." I looked at him in amazement. "Thou hast seen her?" "Yes, many times. I want thee to ask her to the house, where we may have a chance to talk." I sat back in my chair and looked at him, and said within myself, "Was ever mother blessed with such children; what may I next expect?" He gave me a quick look, and came over and took my hand in his, and said, "Now, Mother, do not get excited, and don't look as if the Heavens were going to fall. I— well— thou makest it hard to tell thee, but I want to marry Kah-li, and I would like a chance of seeing her as the foreign men see their wives before they marry them." I said, quite calmly for me, "Thou meanest thou art choosing thy wife instead of allowing thy father and mother to choose her?" He said, "Why, yes; I have to live with her and I ought to choose her." I said nothing— what is the use? I have learned that my men-folk have strong minds, which they certainly must have inherited from thine honourable family. I said that first I would speak to her mother, and if she approved of her daughter's seeing my son in this most unbecoming manner, I would do whatsoever he wished in the matter. I could not wait, but went at once to the house of Wu Tai-tai. We discussed the matter over many cups of tea, and we saw that we are but clouds driven by the winds and we must obey.

She has been here for tea, and I am charmed with her. She is as pretty as a jewel of pure jade; I do not blame my son. She has laughter in her dancing eyes and seems as if she would sing her life away from year to year and see life always through the golden gleam of happy days. She is respectful and modest, and now I feel she is one of the family and I ask her to join us in all our feastings. She came to the feast when we burned the Kitchen God, and joined with us in prayers as he ascended to the great Spirit to tell him of our actions in the past year. I am afraid our young people do not believe o'ermuch in this small God of the Household, who sits so quietly upon his shelf above the kitchen stove for twelve long months, watching all that goes on within the home, then gives his message for good or ill to Him above; but they are too respectful to say ought against it— in my hearing. They must respect the old Gods until they find something better to take their place.

I do not know but that my son is right in this question of his courtship. It is pretty to see them as they wander through the gardens, while we mothers sit upon the balconies and gossip. Their love seems to be as pure as spotless rice and "so long as colour is colour and life is life will the youth with his sublime folly wait for the meeting of his loved one." What matter if the winter days will come to them or if "the snow is always sure to blot out the garden—" today is spring, and love is love and youth is happy.

Thy shameless daughter, Kwei-li.

19

My Dear Mother,

Thy gifts which came by the hand of Tuang-fang are most welcome. We have already drunk of the sun-dried tea, and it brings to thought the sight of the long, laden trays of the fragrant leaves as they lie in the sun on the mountain-side. The rose wine we will use on occasions of special rejoicing; and I thank thee again for the garments which will bring comfort to so many in the coming days of cold. I was glad to see Tuang-fang, and sorry to hear that he, with his brother, are going so far away from home in search of labour. Is there not work enough for our men in the province without going to that land of heat and sickness?

Our people go far in their passion for labour; in search of it they cross land and sea. They are the workers of the world, who sell their labour for a price; and it is only strong men with great self-dependence who are capable of taking a road that is likely never to join again those who speak their language and worship their Gods. What is it that has given these men this marvellous adaptability to all conditions, however hard they may seem? They can live and work in any climate, they are at home in the sandy wastes of our great deserts or in the swamps of the southern countries. They bear the biting cold of northern lands as readily as they labour under the burning sun of Singapore and Java. The more I come out from the courtyard and see our people, the more I admire them; I see the things that are so often lost sight of by those of other lands who seek to study them. They are a philosophical race and bear the most dreadful losses and calamities with wonderful bravery. Nothing daunts them. Behold the family of Tuang-fang: they saw their home ruined at time of flood and began again on the morrow to build on the remaining foundations. They saw their fields burned up by drouth, and took their winter clothing to the pawn-shop to get money to buy seed for the coming spring. They did not complain so long as they could get sufficient food to feed their bodies and the coarse blue cloth with which to clothe them, and when these failed they sent their three strong sons, the best of the family, to the rubber plantations of the South.

We hear so much in the papers here of the "Yellow Peril." If there is a Yellow Peril, it lies in the fact that our men are ready to labour unceasingly for a wage on which most Europeans would starve, and on that pittance they manage to save and become rich and prosperous. They have gone into other lands wherever they have found an opening, and some of the southern countries, like Singapore and the Philippines, owe much of their commercial progress to our people. They are honest and industrious, and until the foreigner began to feel the pinch of competition, until he found that he must work all day and not sleep the hours away if he would be in the race with the man from the Eastern land, he had nothing to say about the character of the man from China. But so soon as he felt the pressure of want because of his sloth, he began to find that the "yellow man" was vicious, and soon his depravity became a by-word. The Chinese were abused because of their virtues rather than their vices, for things for which all other nations are applauded— love of work and economy. It is the industry of our people that offends, because it competes with the half-done work of the white man, who dissipates his time and money.

The men from this land have learned their ways of work at home, where the struggle for existence is hard. Sunrise sees the carpenter and the smith, the shoemaker and the beater of cotton at their labour, and the mid-night cry of the watchman often finds them patiently earning the rice for the morrow's meal. And they have not learned to disobey when told to go to work. There are no strikes as in the foreign countries. Our workmen are obedient, although it is said that they lack in leadership, that nothing is originated within themselves; but they can be taught, and all who employ Chinese labour testify to their ability to follow a good master.

I think, from hearing the gossip from thy son's courtyard, that when China is again peaceful, there will be more chance for the men within her borders, who can then stay beside their fires and earn their food. Our land is a land of fertile soil, of rich minerals, and great rivers. It is said that there are millions and millions of acres on which food or other products can be grown, and that a great part of China may be made one vast garden. The German scientist who is trying to get a coal mine concession from the government told my husband that there were tens of millions of tons of coal of the best quality in China, and that the single province of Shansi could supply the entire world for a thousand years. No wonder the Germans are looking with longing eyes on China! But we want these riches and this labour for our people. If it is worth the time of men of other countries to come to this far-off land in search of what lies beneath our soil, it is worth our while to guard it and keep it for our own.

We hear news of battles and of secret plottings, and I am worried about my son, who is in Canton, the province that seems to be the centre of rebellion and the breeding-place of plots and treachery. I wonder what will be the outcome of it all; if after all this turmoil and bloodshed China will really become a different nation? It is hard to change the habits of a nation, and I think that China will not be changed by this convulsion. The real Chinese will be the same passive, quiet, slow-thinking and slow-moving toiler, not knowing or caring whether his country is a republic or whether he is ruled by the Son of Heaven. He will be a stable, peaceable, law-abiding citizen or subject, with respect for his officials so long as they are not too oppressive; not asking whether the man who rules him is called a governor or a futai, so long as work is plentiful and rice is cheap. These patient, plodding men of China have held together for countless thousands of years, and I am sure that their strength is derived from qualities capable of bearing great strain; and our government, even the government which we are trying so hard to overturn and mould on Western lines, must have suited the country and the people, because nothing ever persists generation after generation, century after century, without being suited to its environment and more or less adapted to the changes which time always brings.

Confucius said, "When I was on a mission to Ch'u State, I saw a litter of young pigs nestling close to their dead mother. After a while they looked at her, then all left the dead body and went off. For their mother did not look at them any more, nor did she seem any more to be of their kind. What they loved was their mother: not the body which contained her, but that which made the body what it was."

That is the way with our country. She may leave the dead forms of her old government, perhaps it will be her misfortune to leave her religion, but the spirit of her government and the spirit of her religion she will always love.

But I must not gossip more with thee over my dearly loved country and her people. I know I talk to thee o'ermuch of politics and the greedy eyes of foreigners which are fixed upon our land, but one cannot live in Shanghai, even behind the women's archway, without hearing, night and day, the things that move this, our world, so strongly. Even my small children play at war, shoot their rebels, build their fortresses and drive the foreigners from off their piles of sand.

I cry to thee, my Mother, because a heart must speak its bitterness, and here our lips are sealed to all. I dare not even tell thy son, my husband, all that passes in my mind as I look from out my window at this fighting, struggling, maddened world that surges round me. We are more than troubled about our son.

Thy daughter, Kwei-li.

20

My Dear Mother,

I send to thee some silken wadding for the lining of thy coat, also a piece of sable to make a scarf for Su-su, and a box of clothing for her new-born son. The children each have written her a letter, and the candles have been lighted before Kwan-yin, to show our joy.

We have a guest, old General Wang, who is on his way to visit with my father. He is of the old, old China, and wags his head most dolefully over the troubles of his country, and says a republic never will succeed. My husband was bewailing the fact of the empty strong-box, and Wang said, "Why don't you do what I did when I was in command of the troops? When money was scarce, I simply stopped a dollar a month from each man's pay, and, lo, there was the money." He was quite shameless in regard to the old-time "squeeze" and said it was necessary. When he was general he received the salary of an ill-paid servant and was expected to keep up the state of a small king. But there were many ways to fill the empty pockets. When a high official was sent to inspect his troops, men were compelled to come from the fields, the coolies to lay down their burdens, the beggar to leave his begging-bowl, and all to stand straight as soldiers with guns within their hands. But when the officer was gone each went his way with a small present in his hand and did not appear again until the frightened official was compelled to sweep the highways and byways to find men enough to agree with lists paid by the government.

But those times are past, and these old-time officials find it safer to retire to homes within their provinces.

He told us of Chung-tai, who was Taotai of our city at one time. Dost thou remember him? He made many millions in the exportation of rice at time of famine. He was asked to go to Peking, and promised a high position. He sent as answer the story of Chung Tzu the philosopher, who was fishing in the Piu when the Prince of Ch'u sent high officials to ask him to take charge of the State. Chung went on fishing and without turning his head said: "I have heard that in Ch'u there is a sacred tortoise which has been dead now some three thousand years, and that the Prince keeps this tortoise carefully enclosed in a chest on the altar of the sacred temple. Now would this tortoise rather be dead and have its remains venerated, or be alive and wagging its tail in the mud?" "It would rather be alive and wagging its tail in the mud," said the officials. "Begone" said Chung. "The tortoise is a symbol of longevity and great wisdom. It would not befit me to aspire to greater wisdom than the tortoise. I, too, prefer the mud."

Chung spoke bravely in sending this reply to Peking; but no sooner was it sent than he gathered his family and his sycee and departed for Shanghai, where he feels more sure of the protection of the foreign settlements than he does of the kindly intentions of His Excellency Yuan toward his dollars.

The children have come home and are clamouring for their supper. They are growing rougher and noisier each day, and, I fear, are spending far too many hours in the servants' courtyard, where they hear of things not seemly for young ears. Canst thou send me Wong-si for a few months? She might be able to keep some order in my household, although I doubt a person of a nature not divine being able to still the many tongues I have now about me.

We send thee love, and greetings to thy new-born great-grandson.

Kwei-li.

21

My Dear Mother,

I have been in the country with my friend Ang Ti-ti. It was the time of pilgrimage to the graves of her family at the temple near Wu-seh. My household gave me many worries, and my husband said it was a time of rest for me, so we took a boat, with only a few servants, as I am tired of chattering women, and spent three long happy days amongst the hills. We sat upon the deck as the boat was slowly drawn along the canal, and watched the valley that autumn now is covering with her colours rare. All the green of the fields is changed. All the gay foliage of the trees upon the hillsides will soon be dead and crumbling. These withered leaves that once waved gaily in the air are lying now in clustered heaps, or fluttering softly to the ground like dull, brown butterflies who are tired with flight. The only touch of colour is on the maple-trees, which still cling with jealous hands to coverings of red and gold. The autumn winds wailed sadly around our cabin windows, and every gust brought desolation to tree and shrub and waving grass. Far away the setting sun turned golden trees to flame, and now and then on the sluggish waters of the canal would drift in lonely splendour a shining leaf that autumn winds had touched and made into a thing of more than beauty.

We anchored the first night by a marshy bank girdled with tall yellow reeds and dwarf bamboo, and from our quiet cabin listened to the rainy gusts that swept the valley. Out of the inky clouds the lightning flashed and lighted up each branch and stem and swaying leaf, revealing to our half-blinded eyes the rain-swept valley; then darkness came with her thick mantle and covered all again.

We discussed the past, the present, and the future; and then, as always when mothers meet, the talk would turn to children. How we are moved by our children! We are like unto the Goddess of the Pine-tree. She came out from her rugged covering and bore a man-child for her husband's house, and then one day the overlord of all that land sent to cut down the pine-tree, that its great trunk might form the rooftree of his temple. At the first blow of the axe the soul glided back into its hiding-place, and the woman was no more. And when it fell, three hundred men could not move it from its place of falling; but her baby came and, putting out his hand, said, "Come," and it followed him quite quietly, gliding to the very doorway of the temple. So do our children lead us with their hands of love.

On the second day we went to the temple to offer incense at the family shrine of Ang Ti-ti. We Chinese ladies love these pilgrimages to these shrines of our ancestors, and it is we who keep up the family worship. We believe that it is from the past that we must learn, and "the past is a pathway which spirits have trodden and made luminous." It is true, as Lafcadio Hearn has written, "We should be haunted by the dead men and women of our race, the ancestors that count in the making of our souls and have their silent say in every action, thought and impulse of our life. Are not our ancestors in very truth our souls? Is not every action the work of the dead who dwell within us? Have not our impulses and our tendencies, our capacities and our weaknesses, our heroisms and our fears, been created by those vanished myriads from whom we received that all-mysterious gift of life? Should we think of that thing which is in each of us and which we call 'I' should it be 'I' or 'they'? What is our pride or shame but the pride or shame of the unseen in that which they have made? And what is our conscience but the inherited sum of countless dead experiences with all things good and evil?"

"In this worship that we give the dead they are made divine. And the thought of this tender reverence will temper with consolation the melancholy that comes with age to all of us. Never in our China are the dead too quickly forgotten; by simple faith they are still thought to dwell among their beloved, and their place within the home remains holy. When we pass to the land of shadows we know that loving lips will nightly murmur our names before the family shrine, that our faithful ones will beseech us in their pain and bless us in their joy. We will not be left alone upon the hillsides, but loving hands will place before our tablet the fruits and flowers and dainty food that we were wont to like, and will pour for us the fragrant cups of tea or amber rice-wine."

"Strange changes are coming upon this land, old customs are vanishing, old beliefs are weakening, the thoughts of today will not be the thoughts of tomorrow; but of all this we will know nothing. We dream that for us as for our mothers the little lamp will burn on through the generations; we see in fancy the yet unborn, the children of our children's children, bowing their tiny heads and making the filial obeisance before the tablets that bear our family name."

This is our comfort, we who feel that "this world is not a place of rest, but where we may now take our little ease, until the land-lord whom we never see, gives our apartment to another guest."

As I said to thee, it is the women who are the preservers of the family worship and who are trying hard to cling to old loved customs. Perhaps it is because we suffer from lack of facility in adapting ourselves to new conditions. We are as fixed as the star in its orbit. Not so much the men of China but we women of the inner courtyards seem to our younger generation to stand an immovable mountain in the pathway of their freedom from the old traditions.

In this course we are only following woman nature. An instinct more powerful than reason seems to tell us that we must preserve the thing we know. Change we fear. We see in the new ideas that our daughters bring from school, disturbers only of our life's ideals. Yet the new thoughts are gathering about our retreats, beating at our doorways, creeping in at the closely shuttered windows, even winning our husbands and our children from our arms. The enclosing walls and the jealously guarded doors of our courtyards are impotent. While we stand a foe of this so-called progress, a guardian of what to us seems womanhood and modesty, the world around us is moving, feeling the impulse of a larger life, broadening its outlook and clothing itself in new expression that we hardly understand. We feel that we cannot keep up with this generation; and, seeing ourselves left behind with our dead Gods, we cry out against the change which is coming to our daughters with the advent of this new education and the knowledge of the outside world. But—.

All happy days must end, and we floated slowly back to the

busy life again. As we came down the canal in the soft moonlight it recalled those other nights to me upon the mountain-side, and as I saw the lights of the city before us I remembered the old poem of Chang Chili Lo:

"The Lady Moon is my lover, My friends are the Oceans four, The Heavens have roofed me over, And the Dawn is my golden door. I would liefer follow a condor, Or the sea-gull soaring from ken, Than bury my Godhead yonder, In the dust and whirl of men."

Thy daughter, Kwei-li.

22

My Dear Mother,

I have not written thee for many days. I came back from my happy country trip to find clouds of sorrow wrapping our home in close embrace. We hear Ting-fang is in deep trouble, and we cannot understand it. He is accused of being in league with the Southern forces. Of course we do not believe it, my son is not a traitor; but black forebodings rise from deeps unknown and the cold trail of fear creeps round my heart.

But I cannot brood upon my fears alone; this world seems full of sorrow. Just now I have stopped my letter to see a woman who was brought to the Yamen for trying to kill her baby daughter. She is alone, has no one to help her in her time of desolation, no rice for crying children, and nothing before her except to sell her daughter to the tea-house. She gave her sleep; and who can blame her?

Mother, send me all that thou canst spare from out thy plenty. I would I could give more. I would be a lamp for those who need a lamp, a bed for those who need a bed; but I am helpless. O, He who hears the wretched when they cry, deign to hear these mothers in their sorrow!

Thy daughter, Kwei-li.

23

I know that thou hast heard the news, as it is in all the papers. Ting-fang is accused of throwing the bomb that killed General Chang. I write to reassure thee that it cannot be true. I know my son. Thou knowest thy family. No Liu could do so foul a deed.

Do not worry; we will send thee all the news. The morrow's tidings will be well, so rest in peace.

Kwei-li.

24, A

I thank thee from my heart for the ten thousand taels tele-graphed for the use of our son. Father has sent fifty thousand taels to be used in obtaining his freedom. I am sure it will not be needed, as my son is not the culprit. And if he were, it is not the olden time when a life could be bought for a few thousand ounces of silver, no matter how great the crime. We will not bribe the Courts of Law, even for our son.

But I am sure it will pass with the night's darkness, and we will wake to find it all a dream. I know, my mother's heart assures me, that my boy is innocent.

Do not speak or think of coming down. We will let thee know at once all news.

Kwei-li

24, B

[*Telegram*] We are leaving tonight for Canton.

25

We are entering Canton. The night denies me sleep, and my brain seems beating like the tireless shuttles upon a weaving-loom. I cannot rest, but walk the deck till the moon fades from the dawn's pale sky, and the sun shows rose-coloured against the morning's grey. Across the river a temple shines faintly through its ring of swaying bamboo, and the faint light glistens on the water dripping from the oars that bring the black-sailed junks with stores of vegetables for all that greedy city of living people. The mists cling lovingly to the hill-tops, while leaves from giant banyan-trees sway idly in the morning wind, and billows of smoke, like dull, grey spirits, roll up-ward and fade into a mist of clouded jade, touched with the golden fingers of the rising sun.

I see it all with eyes that do not see, because the creeping hours I count until I find my son.

26

Ting-fang has been tried and found guilty. The runners have brought me hour by hour the news; and even his father can see nothing that speaks in favour of his innocence. It is known and he confesses to having been with the men who are the plotters in this uprising. He was with the disloyal officers only a few hours before the bomb was thrown, but of the actual deed he insists that he knows nothing. All evidence points to his guilt. Even the official who sentenced him, a life-long friend of ours, said in the open court that it hurt him sorely to condemn a man bearing the great name of Liu, because of what his father and his father's father had been to China, but in times such as these an example must be made; and all the world is now looking on to see what will be done.

I will write thee and telegraph thee further news; I can say no more at present; my heart is breaking.

Kwei-li.

27

A man came to us secretly last night and offered to effect my son's escape for fifty thousand taels. He said that arrangements could be made to get him out of the country— and we have refused! We told him we could give no answer until the morning, and I walked the floor the long night through, trying to find the pathway just.

We cannot do it. China is at the parting of the ways; and if we, her first officials, who are taking the stand upon the side of justice and new ideas of honour, do not remain firm in hours of great temptation, what lesson have we to give to them who follow where we lead? It ust not be said that our first acts were those of bribery and corruption. If my son is a traitor, we let him pay. He must give his life upon the altar of new China. We cannot buy his life. We are of the house of Liu, and our name must stand, so that, through the years to come, it will inspire those who follow us to live and die for China, the country that we love.

28

My Mother,

From the red dawn until the dense night fell, and all the hours of darkness through, have my weary feet stumbled on in hopeless misery, waiting, listening for the guns that will tell to me my son is gone. At sunset a whispered message of hope was brought, then vanished quite again, and I have walked the lengthened reach of the great courtyard, watching as, one by one, the lanterns die and the world is turning into grey. Far away toward the rice-fields the circling gulls rise, flight on flight, and hover in the blue, then fly away to life and happiness in the great beyond. In the distance, faint blue smoke curls from a thousand dwellings of people who are rising and will greet their sons, while mine lies dead. Oh, I thought that tears were human only, yet I see each blade of shining grass weighed down with dewdrop tears that glimmer in the air. Even the grass would seem all sorrow filled as is my heart.

The whole night through the only sound has been the long-drawn note of the bamboo flute, as the seller passes by, and the wind that wailed and whistled and seemed to bring with it spirits of the other world who came and taunted me that I did not save my son. Why, why did I not save him! What is honour, what is this country, this fighting, quarrelling, maddened country, what is our fame, in comparison to his dear life? Why did we not accept the offer of escape! It was ours to give or take; we gave, and I repent— O God, how I repent! My boy, my boy! I will be looking for his face in all my dreams and find despair.

....

Dost thou remember how he came to me in answer to the Towers of Prayer I raised when my first-born slept so deep a sleep he could not be wakened even by the voice of his mother? But that sorrow passed and I rose to meet a face whose name is memory. At last I knew it was not kindness to mourn so for my dead. Over the River of Tears their silent road is, and when mothers weep too long, the flood of that river rises, and their souls cannot pass but must wander to and fro. But to those whom they leave with empty arms they are never utterly gone. They sleep in the darkest cells of tired hearts and busy brains, to come at echo of a voice that recalls the past.

....

My sleeve is wet with bitter rain; but tears cannot blot out the dream visions that memory wakes, and the dead years answer to my call. I see my boy, my baby, who was the gift of kindly Gods. When I first opened my eyes upon him, I closed them to all the world besides, and my soul rested in peace beside the jewel within its cradle. The one sole wish of my heart was to be near him, to sit close by his side, to have him day by day within my happy sight, and to lay my cheek upon his rose-tipped feet at night. The sun's light seemed more beautiful where it touched him, and the moon that lit my Heaven was his eyes.

As he grew older he was fond of asking questions to which none but the Gods could give reply, and I answered as only mothers will. When he wished to play I laid aside my work to play with him, and when he tired and wished to rest, I told him stories of the past. At evening when the lamps were lighted I taught him the words of the evening prayer, and when he slept I brought my work close by his cradle and watched the still sweetness of his face. Sometimes he would smile in his dreams, and I knew that Kwan-yin the Divine was playing shadow-play with him, and I would murmur a silent prayer to the Mother of all Mercies to protect my treasure and keep him from all harm.

....

I can see my courtyard in far Sezchuan; and in the wooden box within my bedroom are all his baby-clothes. There are the shoes with worn-out toes and heels that tried so hard to confine restless, eager feet; the cap with Buddha and his saints, all broken and tarnished where tiny, baby teeth have left their marks; and, Mother, dost thou remember when we made him clothing like the soldier at the Yamen? And the bamboo that the gateman polished he carried for a gun...

O my son, my son! How can I rise to begin the bitter work of life through the twilights yet to come!

29

How can I tell thee, Mother mine, of the happiness within my heart! It is passed; it was but a dream, a mirage. He is here, my boy, his hand in mine, his cheek against my cheek; he is mine own again, my boy, my man-child, my son.

It was not he; the culprit has been found; and in the golden morning light my son stood free before me. I cannot write thee more at present, I am so filled with joy. What matter if the sun shines on wrinkles and white hair, the symbol of the fulness of my sorrow— I have mine own again!

30

My Dear Mother,

I can talk to thee more calmly, and I know thou hungerest for full news. Dost thou remember Liang Tai-tai, she whom I wrote thee was so anxious for the mercy of the Gods that she spent her time in praying instead of looking after household duties and her son? He was the one who tried to pass the Dark Water and I talked to him and we sent him to the prefect at Canton. It was he who found the man for whom my son was accused. It seemed he felt he owed us much for helping him in his time of trouble, and now he has repaid.

I feel that I have laughed too oft at Liang Tai-tai and her Gods, but now I will go with her from temple shrine to temple shrine. I will buy for her candles, incense, spirit money, until the Gods look down in wonder from their thrones. I am so filled with gratitude that when I see my friend, I will fall before her feet and bathe them with my happy tears for having trod the path of motherhood and given to the world a man-child, who has saved for me my son.

Kwei-li.

31

My Mother,

We are home, and have not written thee for long, but have telegraphed thee twice daily, so that thou hast been assured that all is well.

We found our dear one, our Li-ti, bending o'er her babe, holding it safely, nestling it, murmuring, softly, whispers of mother love. This son, born in the hour of trouble and despair, is a token of the happiness to come, of the new life that will come forth from grief and sorrow.

He has learned a lesson, this boy of mine, and he will walk more carefully, guard more surely his footsteps, now he is the father of a son.

Kwei-li.

32

O Mother of graciousness, we are coming to thee! When all the hills are white with blossoms, we shall set forth, our eager hearts and souls one great, glad longing for the sight of thee standing in the archway, searching with earnest gaze the road, listening for the bearers' footsteps as we mount the hillside.

We leave this place of trial and turmoil. I want my children to come within the shelter of thy compound walls, where safety lies; and with the "shell of forgetfulness" clasped tightly in our hands, we will forget these days of anguish and despair. Then only, when my dear ones are far from here, shall my soul obtain the peace it craves, forgetful of the hostile, striving, plotting treachery of this foreign world I fear.

We are coming home to thee, Mother of my husband, and I have learned in life's great, bitter school that the joy of my Chinese woman-hood is to stand within the sheltered courtyard, with my family close about me, and my son's son in my arms.

Kwei-li.

The End

www.ingramcontent.com/pod-product-compliance
Lightning Source LLC
Chambersburg PA
CBHW030016290326
41934CB00005B/362